Physics!
BEST
SCIENCE
PROJECTS

Electricity and Magnetism Science Fair Projects

Using Batteries, Balloons, and Other Hair-Raising Stuff

Robert Gardner

Enslow Publishers, Inc.

40 Industrial Road   PO Box 38
Box 398   Aldershot
Berkeley Heights, NJ 07922   Hants GU12 6BP
USA   UK

http://www.enslow.com

Library of Congress Cataloging-in-Publication Data

Gardner, Robert, 1929–
    Electricity and magnetism science fair projects using batteries,
    balloons, and other hair-raising stuff / Robert Gardner.
        v. cm. — (Physics! best science projects)
    Includes bibliographical references and index.
    Contents: Static electricity : charges at rest — Moving charges — Magnets and
magnetic fields — Magnetism from electricity — Electricity magnets and motors —
Electricity and chemistry.
    ISBN 0-7660-2127-0 (hardcover)
    1. Electricity—Experiments—Juvenile literature. 2. Magnetism—Experiments—
Juvenile literature. 3. Science projects—Juvenile literature. [1. Electricity—Experiments.
2. Magnetism—Experiments. 3. Experiments. 4. Science projects.] I. Title.
    II. Series.
    QC533.G37 2004
    537'.078—dc22
                                2003026960

Printed in the United States of America

10 9 8 7 6 5 4 3 2 1

To Our Readers: We have done our best to make sure all Internet Addresses in this
book were active and appropriate when we went to press. However, the author and the
publisher have no control over and assume no liability for the material available on those
Internet sites or on other Web sites they may link to. Any comments or suggestions can
be sent by e-mail to comments@enslow.com or to the address on the back cover.

Illustration Credits: Tom LaBaff

Cover Photo: Copyright © 2002–2004 Art Today, Inc.

AET-5649

Contents

Introduction

Physics is the part of science that deals with matter and energy. You and the world around you are made up of matter. All activity involves energy. By studying physics, you can unlock the secrets of matter and energy.

Electricity and magnetism are fundamental forms of energy. Try to imagine what your life would be like without electricity. Industrial and commercial work would be done in horse-and-buggy ways. There would be no television, computers, or CDs. You would be reading this book by candlelight.

The significance of magnetism is more elusive. However, by the time you finish this book, you will see that without magnetism, the electricity we take for granted would not exist.

In this book you will find projects and experiments that show how electricity and magnetism work. Most of the materials you will need can be found in your home. Several of the experiments may require items that you can buy in a supermarket, a hobby or toy shop, a hardware store, or one of the science supply companies listed in the appendix. Some projects may call for articles that you may be able to borrow from your school's science department. Occasionally, you will need someone to help you with an experiment that requires more than one pair of hands. It would be best if you work with friends or adults who enjoy experimenting as much as you do. In that way you will both enjoy what you are doing. **If any danger is involved in doing an experiment, a warning in bold type will let you know.**

In some cases, to avoid any danger to you, you will be asked to work with an adult. Please do so. Do not take any chances that could lead to an injury.

Like any good scientist, you will find it useful to record your ideas, notes, data, and anything you can conclude from your experiments in a notebook. By so doing, you can keep track of the information you gather and the conclusions you reach. It will allow you to refer to experiments you have done and help you in doing other projects in the future.

SCIENCE FAIRS

Some of the projects in this book are followed by a section called Science Project Ideas. These project ideas are a good place to start thinking of your own science fair projects. However, judges at such fairs do not reward projects or experiments that are simply copied from a book. For example, a diagram or model of an incandescent lightbulb would not impress judges; however, a series of experiments designed to test the longevity of lightbulb filaments made from different materials would gain serious consideration.

Science fair judges tend to reward creative thought and imagination. It is difficult to be creative or imaginative unless you are really interested in your project. Be sure to choose a subject that appeals to you. And before you jump into a project, consider, too, your own talents and the cost of materials you will need.

If you decide to use a project found in this book for a science fair, you should find ways to modify or extend it. This should not be difficult because you will probably discover that as you do these projects new ideas for experiments will come to mind—experiments that could make excellent science fair projects, particularly because the ideas are your own and are interesting to you.

If you decide to enter a science fair and have never done so before, look at some of the books listed in the further reading section. Some of these books deal specifically with science fairs. They will provide plenty of hints and useful information that will enable you to avoid the pitfalls that sometimes plague first-time entrants. You will learn how to prepare appealing reports that include charts and graphs, how to set up and display your work, how to present your project, and how to relate to judges and visitors.

SAFETY FIRST

Most of the projects included in this book are perfectly safe. However, the following safety rules are well worth reading before you start any project.

✓ Do any experiments or projects, whether from this book or of your own design, under the supervision of a science teacher or other knowledgeable adult.

✓ Read all instructions carefully before proceeding with a project. If you have questions, check with your supervisor before going any further.

✓ Maintain a serious attitude while conducting experiments. Fooling around can be dangerous to you and to others.

✓ Wear approved safety goggles when you are working with a flame or doing anything that might cause injury to your eyes.

✓ Do not eat or drink while experimenting.

✓ Have a first-aid kit nearby while you are experimenting.

✓ Do not put your fingers or any object other than properly designed electrical connectors into electrical outlets.

✓ Never let water droplets come in contact with a hot lightbulb.

✓ Never experiment with household electricity except under the supervision of a knowledgeable adult.

Chapter 1

Static Electricity: Charges at Rest

Since ancient times, people have known a strange fact about amber. Amber—a brownish gold gem—is a fossil material made by trees. When rubbed with cloth, a piece of amber can attract and even lift light objects. In the sixteenth century, William Gilbert, an English scientist, demonstrated that substances other than amber had similar properties. Gilbert referred to materials that could attract light objects when rubbed as *electrics*. The word *electrics* comes from the Greek word for amber (*elektron*).

The experiments in this chapter are related to Gilbert's electrics. These experiments should be done when there is little humidity (*damp* air). Low humidity is most common in the winter because cold air cannot hold very much moisture. Your first experience with static electricity probably took place on a winter's day. You walked across a carpet wearing rubber-soled shoes. You reached for a metal door handle and *wham*! you felt a shock and perhaps saw a spark jump between your hand and the metal. Or perhaps you took off a sweater in a dark room and saw sparks moving between the sweater and your body. These experiences result from static electricity, the buildup of electric charges on the surface of materials such as wool and plastics. Unlike the electric charges that flow along wires, static charges are at rest.

In this chapter, you will find out how to create charges, discover ways to detect them, and investigate the different kinds of charges. In later chapters, you will find that these charges can move. Their motion can be controlled, and the energy they possess can be utilized. But you can begin by giving some objects a static charge.

Experiment 1.1

Getting Charged

Materials

- ✓ 2 rubber balloons
- ✓ 2 twist ties
- ✓ 2 strings about 30 cm (1 ft) long
- ✓ clear plastic tape
- ✓ door frame or table
- ✓ woolen cloth or paper towel

- ✓ 2 plastic rulers
- ✓ thread
- ✓ glass test tube or a glass rod
- ✓ various plastic objects, wooden pencils, balloons, and other objects
- ✓ silk, rayon, and nylon

Blow up two rubber balloons. Seal them shut with twist ties, and connect both to strings about 30 cm (1 ft) long. Use tape to suspend one balloon from a door frame or table as shown in Figure 1a. Rub this balloon thoroughly with a piece of woolen cloth or a paper towel. Then rub the second balloon in the same way. Hold the second balloon by its string and slowly bring it near the suspended balloon. What happens? At what distance between the balloons can you detect a change? What happens as the distance between the balloons decreases?

Next, bring the piece of wool or the paper towel with which you rubbed the balloon near the suspended balloon. What happens?

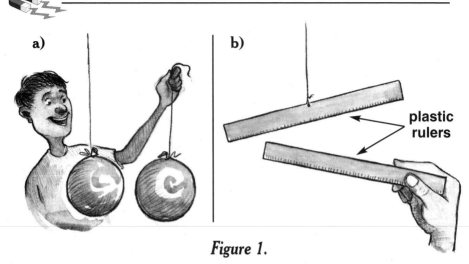

Figure 1.

a) Suspend a balloon with string. Then rub that balloon and a second with a woolen cloth or a paper towel. Bring the second balloon close to the suspended balloon. What happens? b) Suspend a plastic ruler from a thread. Rub the ruler with a woolen cloth. Rub a second plastic ruler with a woolen cloth. What happens when you bring the second ruler near the suspended one?

A similar experiment can be done using plastic rulers. Suspend a plastic ruler by a thread as shown in Figure 1b. Rub the ruler briskly with a woolen cloth. Rub a second plastic ruler with the same woolen cloth. Like the balloons, both rulers were charged in the same way; therefore, we might expect both rulers to have the same kind of charge. What do you predict will happen when you bring the second ruler close to the first one? Try it! Were you right?

What do you predict will happen when you bring the woolen cloth near the suspended ruler? Again, try it to see if your prediction was right.

From your experiments with the charged balloons and rulers, you can see that charged objects exert a force on one another. When the charges on two objects are the same, do they attract or repel one another? How is the force related to the distance between the charged objects?

Once more, recharge the suspended ruler with a woolen cloth. This time rub a glass test tube or a glass rod with the woolen cloth. Then bring the glass near the charged suspended ruler. What happens this time? How can you tell that the charge on the glass is not the same as the charge on the ruler?

Repeat this experiment a number of times using different materials and different cloths. For example, try charging various plastic objects, wooden pencils, balloons, and other objects with silk, rayon, and nylon as well as woolen cloths and paper towels. Bring each charged object near the charged suspended ruler. What do you find? How many kinds of charge does there seem to be?

Here is a different way to charge objects. Take two strips of clear plastic tape, each about 15 cm (6 in) long. Fold a short length at each end of both strips to make a tab you can grasp. This will keep the tape from sticking to your fingers. Place the sticky side of one strip on the nonsticky side of the other strip. Next hold the strips by their tabs and pull them apart. What happens when you slowly bring the two strips near one another? How do the charges on the two strips compare? Are they the same or different? How can you tell?

Science Project Ideas

- Suppose you add a third strip of sticky tape to two strips like those you put together in the last part of Experiment 1.1. (Place the sticky side of the third strip on the nonsticky side of the second.) How do the charges on each strip compare when you pull them apart one by one? Can you explain what you observe?

- Sprinkle some salt crystals on a dark sheet of paper. Hold a charged balloon above the crystals. Slowly lower the balloon toward the crystals. What happens? Can you explain what you observe?

BENJAMIN FRANKLIN AND STATIC ELECTRICITY

Benjamin Franklin was one of this country's founding fathers. He, like Thomas Jefferson, was involved in science as well as civic affairs. Franklin did experiments similar to those you have just done. He decided that there are two kinds of electric charge, which he called positive (+) and negative (–). He defined positive charge as the charge found on a glass rod rubbed with silk. He defined negative charge as the charge found on a rubber rod rubbed with fur. His experimental results led him to conclude that objects with the same charge repel one another; objects with different charges (one positive, one negative) attract each other. His definition of the sign (positive or negative) of the electric charge on an electrically charged object is still used by physicists today.

Based on the experiments you did, do you agree with Franklin's conclusion?

How do you think Franklin determined whether an object was positively or negatively charged?

Experiment 1.2

Inducing Charge

Materials

✓ balloons

✓ twist tie

✓ woolen cloth or paper towel

✓ wall

✓ a friend

✓ paper to tear up

✓ plastic ruler

✓ bubble wand

✓ bubble-making solution

✓ faucet

Blow up a balloon. Seal its neck with a twist tie. Charge the balloon by rubbing it with a woolen cloth or a paper towel. Place the balloon against a wall. It will stick to the wall.

Rub another balloon with a paper towel or woolen cloth. Then hold it above a friend's head. What happens to your friend's hair?

Tear a small piece of paper into tiny pieces. Then charge a plastic ruler by rubbing it with a woolen cloth or a paper towel. Bring the charged ruler close to the bits of paper. What happens?

Dip a bubble wand in some bubble-making solution. Blow some bubbles. As the bubbles fall, bring a charged plastic ruler near them. What happens?

Charge the ruler again. Then hold the ruler near a very thin stream of water flowing from a faucet. What happens to the stream of water?

In the experiments you have just done, you did not charge the wall, your friend's hair, the bits of paper, the bubbles, or the water. Nevertheless, the charged balloon stuck to the wall, the other charged balloon attracted your friend's hair, the tiny pieces of paper were attracted to the ruler, and so was the thin stream of water.

The electrical attractions you saw can be explained by what is called induction. Suppose the balloon carried negative (–) charge. When you placed it against the wall, negative charges in the wall were repelled and moved away from the balloon. They were *induced* to move away by the negative charges on the balloon. This left positive charges on the wall's surface, and you know that opposite charges attract. A similar thing happened when you brought the charged ruler near the bits of paper and the bubbles.

The stream of water was attracted to the ruler for a somewhat different reason. One side of a molecule of water has a slight negative charge, the other side has a slight positive charge. Scientists call this a polar molecule. If the ruler carried negative charge, the positive sides of the water molecules were attracted to the ruler. The attractive force between the ruler and the molecules caused the stream to be pulled toward the ruler. Of course, the negative sides of the molecules were repelled by the ruler. However, the molecules turned so that the positive ends would be closer to the ruler. As you have seen, the force is less at greater distances. Therefore, the attractive force will be greater than the repelling force, causing the water to move toward the ruler.

Experiment 1.3

Detecting Charge: An Electroscope

Materials

- ✓ **an adult**
- ✓ paper clip
- ✓ match or candle
- ✓ clear plastic cup
- ✓ scissors
- ✓ thin aluminum foil
- ✓ table or counter
- ✓ small nail
- ✓ clay
- ✓ plastic ruler
- ✓ woolen cloth or paper towel

An electroscope is an instrument that can be used to detect electric charge. It can also be used to determine whether an object is charged positively (+) or negatively (−).

You can build a simple electroscope using ordinary, inexpensive materials. To begin, **ask an adult** to make a hole through the bottom of a clear plastic cup. This can be done by heating the end of a partially opened paper clip with a match or candle flame as shown in Figure 2a. The hot paper clip can then be pushed through the bottom of the plastic cup.

While the paper clip is cooling, use scissors to prepare two small strips of aluminum foil. Each piece should be about 4 cm x 1 cm (1½ in by ⅜ in). Use the cooled paper clip to make a hole near one end of each strip. Now open the paper clip so that it has a J shape. Hold the paper clip inside the inverted cup. Push the long side of the paper clip through the hole in the bottom of the cup. Slide the holes in the two aluminum strips over the bent end of the paper clip. (See Figure 2b.) The aluminum strips are called the leaves of the electroscope.

Set the inverted cup on a table or counter. Roll up a piece of aluminum foil into a small ball. Use a nail to make a hole in the aluminum ball. Then slide the hole in the ball onto the upper end of the paper clip, as shown in Figure 2c. Be sure the aluminum strips do not touch the table. Then seal the paper clip to the cup with a lump of clay, and your electroscope is ready for use.

Rub a plastic ruler with a woolen cloth or a paper towel. Slowly, bring the ruler near, but not touching, the aluminum ball. What happens to the two aluminum leaves?

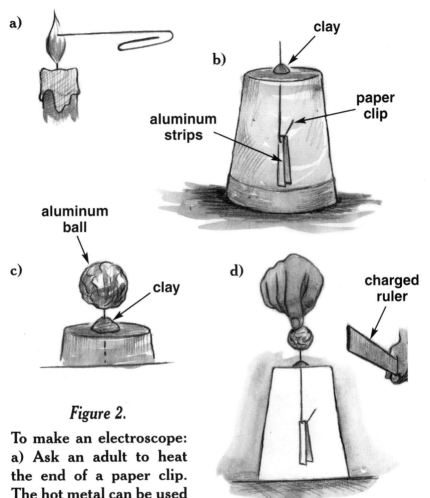

Figure 2.

To make an electroscope:
a) Ask an adult to heat the end of a paper clip. The hot metal can be used to make a hole in the bottom of a clear plastic cup. b) Partially open the cooled paper clip. Extend the straight end through the hole in the cup. Add two small aluminum strips to the bent end of the paper clip. c) Put an aluminum foil ball on the upper end of the paper clip. Seal the paper clip to the cup with clay. d) What happens if you touch an electroscope, bring a charged object near (not touching) the electroscope, remove your finger, and then remove the charged object?

Using what you know about induction, can you explain the behavior of the leaves? How will the charge on the leaves compare with the charge on the plastic ruler?

Next, charge the ruler again and hold it in one hand. Before you bring the charged ruler near the electroscope, place a finger of your other hand on the aluminum ball at the top of the electroscope, as shown in Figure 2d. Bring the ruler toward the top of the electroscope. Then remove your finger from the ball. Next, move the ruler away from the ball. What happens to the leaves? Can you explain why?

Now, slowly bring the ruler toward the aluminum ball again. What happens to the leaves? What does this tell you about the charge on the leaves? Is the sign of the charge on the ruler the same or the opposite of that on the leaves? How do you know?

Science Project Idea

- Investigate the various types of electroscopes. (They can be made in a variety of ways.) Draw diagrams to show how they are alike and how they differ.

Experiment 1.4

Some Static Effects

Materials

- ✓ old pair of panty hose
- ✓ plastic bag
- ✓ plastic comb
- ✓ paper
- ✓ aluminum foil
- ✓ plastic wrap
- ✓ tape
- ✓ Ping-Pong ball
- ✓ plastic ruler

- ✓ paper towel
- ✓ flat piece of clear glass or rigid plastic
- ✓ 2 thin books
- ✓ woolen cloth or paper towel
- ✓ newspaper
- ✓ scissors

Here are a number of experiments that are like magic tricks. See Figure 3.

a) Hold an old pair of panty hose against a wall. Rub the hose briskly with a plastic bag for a few seconds. Release the hose. Do they stick to the wall?

Remove the hose from the wall and hold them from the waistband. What do you notice about the shape of the hose?

b) Use a plastic comb to comb your hair. Then hold the comb near some tiny pieces of paper. What happens? Repeat the experiment using bits of aluminum foil and plastic wrap.

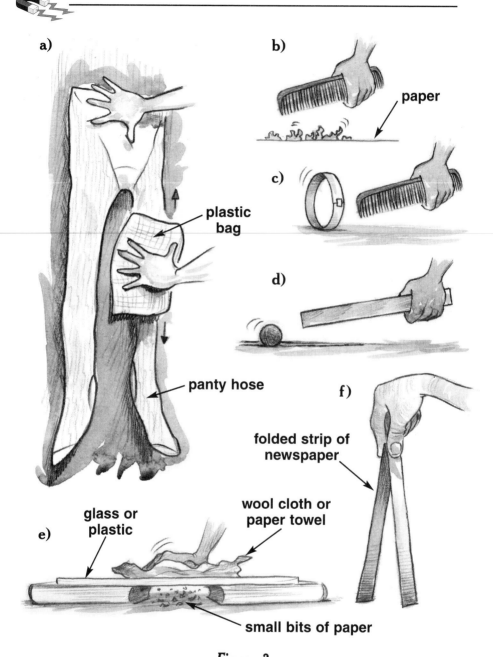

Figure 3.

These experiments demonstrate static electric effects.

c) Cut a strip of paper about 10 cm (4 in) long and 3 cm (1 in) wide. Roll the paper into a narrow cylinder and tape the ends together. Lay the cylinder on its side so that it looks like a wheel. Comb your hair with a plastic comb. What happens when you hold the comb near the paper wheel?

d) For a similar effect, place a Ping-Pong ball on a level surface. Rub a plastic ruler with a paper towel and hold it near the ball. What happens?

e) Tear a small sheet of paper into tiny pieces. Place them under a piece of clear glass or rigid plastic resting on two thin books. Rub the glass with a woolen cloth or paper towel. Watch the paper bits begin to dance.

f) Cut a long strip about 3 cm (1 in) wide from a newspaper. Fold the strip in half. Hold the strip at its fold with the free ends below. Use the thumb and index fingers of your other hand to stroke the two halves of the strip. Why do the two halves fly apart after stroking even though you bring them together when you stroke them?

Chapter 2

Moving Charges

In Chapter 1 you saw that electric charges can be separated. For example, a rubber balloon acquires charge when rubbed with a woolen cloth. The cloth acquires the opposite charge. Because the charges on these objects are at rest, they are referred to as static charge. In this chapter, you will investigate charges that move.

Figures 4a and 4b demonstrate how we know that charges can move. One electroscope has been charged negatively by touching it with a rubber rod that has been rubbed with fur. A second electroscope is positively charged. It has been touched with a glass rod that was rubbed with silk. If these

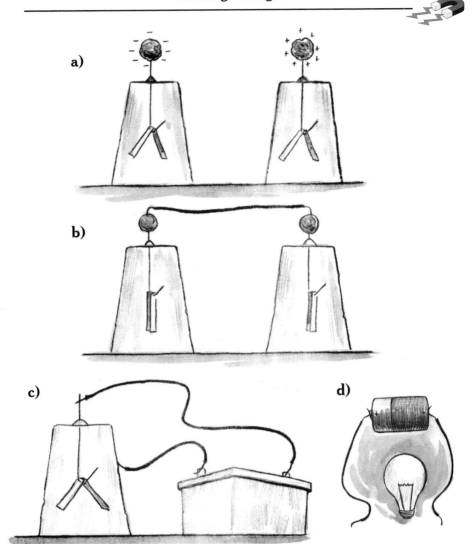

Figure 4.

a) One electroscope is negatively charged. A second electroscope is positively charged. b) When the two electroscopes are connected by an insulated wire with bare ends, the electroscopes discharge. c) A battery can be used to charge an electroscope. d) Can you light a flashlight bulb by touching it with two wires connected to a D cell?

two electroscopes are connected by an insulated wire, both electroscopes discharge (lose their charge). In order to discharge, the charges must have moved from one electroscope to the other. This experiment does not tell us whether positive charges flow to negative charges, negative charges flow to positive charges, or both types of charge move. But it does show that one or both kinds of charge can move from one place to another.

Of course, it is not practical to keep charging electroscopes in order to obtain moving charges. Normally, we use batteries or generators to move charge. A battery is a device that can produce an electric current, a flow of electric charge. Figure 4c shows how a battery can be used to force charge onto an electroscope. In a later chapter, you will investigate how batteries and generators work.

In this chapter, you will move charges and create electric circuits by using batteries. An electric circuit is a complete path along which charges may flow from one pole of a battery to the other. The electric circuits you will make consist of a battery, wires along which charges move, and various devices such as lightbulbs and motors that will react to current from the battery.

Experiment 2.1

A Simple Electric Circuit

Materials

✓ **an adult**

✓ 2 insulated wires about 15 cm (6 in) long

✓ wire stripper or knife

✓ a partner

✓ D cell (flashlight battery)

✓ flashlight bulb

Obtain two insulated wires, each about 15 cm (6 in) long. **Ask an adult** to strip away about 3 cm (1 in) of insulation from each end of the wires. Have a partner hold one end of each of the two wires firmly against the metal ends of the D cell (flashlight battery), as shown in Figure 4d. **Your partner's fingers should not touch the bare wire or the battery poles.** The poles of the cell are probably marked + (positive) and − (negative). If not, the end with the small cylindrical projection is the positive pole. While your partner holds the ends of the two wires against the poles of the D cell, bring the other ends of the wires to the bulb. **Do not touch the bare wires or the metal on the bulb.** At what two places do you have to touch the bulb to make it light?

You know how to connect the bulb to the battery using two wires to make a circuit. How can you light the bulb using just one wire to form the circuit?

Science Project Ideas

- Take a flashlight apart. Can you figure out how it works?

- Build a flashlight of your own design.

Experiment 2.2

Building Circuits

Materials

- ✓ **an adult**
- ✓ paper clips
- ✓ wire stripper
- ✓ thumbtacks
- ✓ D cell
- ✓ soft wood block

- ✓ insulated wires (with alligator clips if available)
- ✓ battery holders and bulb holders
- ✓ strong, wide rubber bands
- ✓ clothespins

Holding wires against battery poles and bulbs is a clumsy and tiring way to build electric circuits. If you have battery holders, bulb holders, and wires with alligator clips like those shown in Figure 5a, you can assemble circuits quickly. If you do not have this equipment, you can make your own from wood, rubber bands, paper clips, thumbtacks, and clothespins (see Figure 5b).

If you build your own equipment, put the bare end of a wire under the thumbtack in your soft-wood bulb holder. Press the

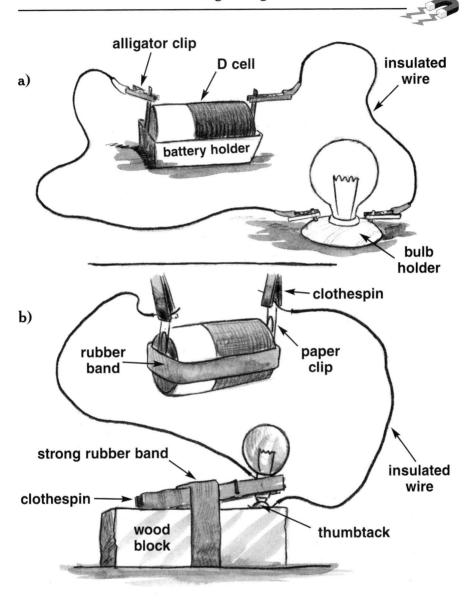

Figure 5.

a) An electric circuit is easy to build if you have battery and bulb holders and wires with alligator clips. b) You can make your own battery and bulb holders using paper clips, rubber bands, thumbtacks, wood blocks, and clothespins.

thumbtack firmly against the wood. This will hold the wire in place and make it unnecessary to move it. The clothespin holding the bulb can then be fixed to the wood block with a strong rubber band. The metal tab at the bottom of the bulb should rest firmly against the thumbtack. A second wire can be inserted between the clothespin and the metal that surrounds the bulb just below the glass part of the bulb.

A battery holder can be made from a strong, wide rubber band that holds paper clips against the poles of a D cell. Clothespins can be used to hold the bare ends of wires against the paper clips.

Most diagrams of electrical circuits do not show all the details of the equipment that you see in Figure 5. Instead a simple code is used. A bulb, for example, is represented by a circle with a zigzag line across it. The circle represents the glass part of the bulb; the zigzag line represents the thin filament that glows when charge flows through it. The various symbols used to represent parts of a circuit are shown in Figure 6.

Use the symbols in Figure 6 to build the circuits shown in Figure 7. In Figure 7d, two D cells can be connected head to tail by using a somewhat longer rubber band or by using a wire to connect the positive (+) pole of one D cell to the negative (–) pole, or terminal, of a second.

In Figure 7b, the D cell has been turned around from its position in 7a. Does turning the cell around affect the brightness of the bulb?

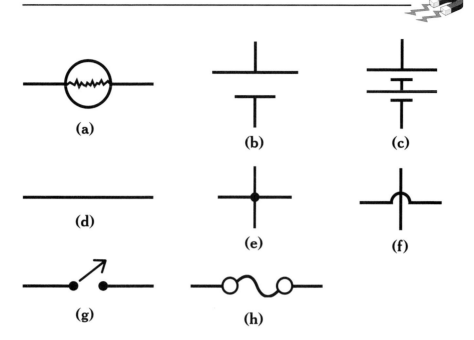

Figure 6.

In drawing electric circuits, the parts may be represented by these symbols. a) a bulb; b) an electric cell (a battery); c) two cells connected head (+) to tail (–); d) a wire; e) wires that are joined; f) wires that cross but are not joined; g) a switch; h) a fuse.

In Figure 7c, a second bulb has been added to the circuit shown in 7a. Does adding a second bulb affect the brightness of the bulbs?

In Figure 7d, a second D cell has been added. Does the addition of a second electric cell affect the brightness of the bulb?

How does the brightness of the two bulbs in Figure 7e compare with the brightness of the bulb in Figure 7a?

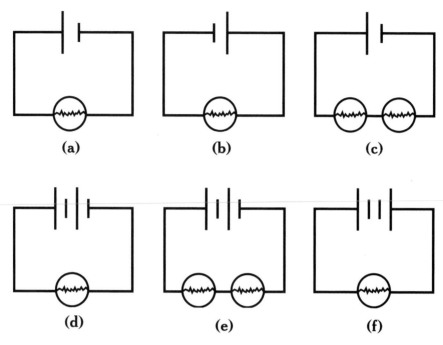

Figure 7.

Use the symbols shown in Figure 6 to build each of the six circuits shown here.

Do you think the bulb in Figure 7f will light? Why or why not? Try it.

Science Project Idea

● Design and build some battery and bulb holders of your own.

Experiment 2.3

Series and Parallel Circuits

Materials

✓ 3 flashlight bulbs   ✓ battery holder
✓ 3 bulb holders   ✓ insulated wires
✓ 2 D cells

Arrange three flashlight bulbs as shown in Figure 8a. When bulbs are arranged in this way, they are said to be wired in series, one after the other. After you have built the circuit, connect it to two D cells in series, as shown.

What happens if you unscrew one of the bulbs? Does it matter which one you unscrew? How can you explain what you have observed?

Now build the circuit shown in Figure 8b. When bulbs are arranged side by side like those in Figure 8b, they are said to be wired in parallel. Why do you think they are said to be wired in parallel? After you have built this parallel circuit, unscrew one of the bulbs. What happens? Does it matter which bulb you unscrew? How can you explain what you have observed?

Build the circuits shown in Figure 8c. Are these bulbs in series or in parallel? How can you find out?

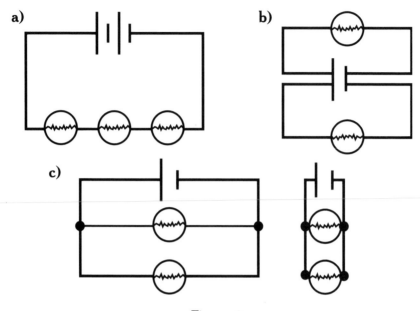

Figure 8.

a) A circuit with three lightbulbs wired in series. b) A circuit with two lightbulbs wired in parallel. c) Are the bulbs in these circuits wired in series or in parallel?

Science Project Idea

● How do you know that the circuit elements in your home or school are wired in parallel? What would happen if they were wired in series?

Experiment 2.4

Switches

Materials

- ✓ 3 small blocks of soft wood
- ✓ thumbtacks
- ✓ paper clips
- ✓ ruler
- ✓ insulated wires
- ✓ household wall switch (obtain from hardware store)

In your house, you use a switch to turn a light on or off. You can make a simple switch to insert in a circuit using a small block of wood, two thumbtacks, and a paper clip (see Figure 9a). Bend a paper clip into an S shape. Push two thumbtacks partway into the wood. They should be about 5 cm (2 in) apart. Wrap the bare ends of two separate wires around the thumbtacks. Push one of the thumbtacks down firmly to hold the wire in place. Slide one end of the paper clip under the second thumbtack before you push it firmly into the wood. You can close the switch by pushing the bent end of the paper clip down onto the head of the first thumbtack. Open the switch by releasing the paper clip.

Now build the circuit shown in Figure 9b. Use the switch to turn the light on and off. How is this switch different from the ones you find in your home?

a)

b)

c)

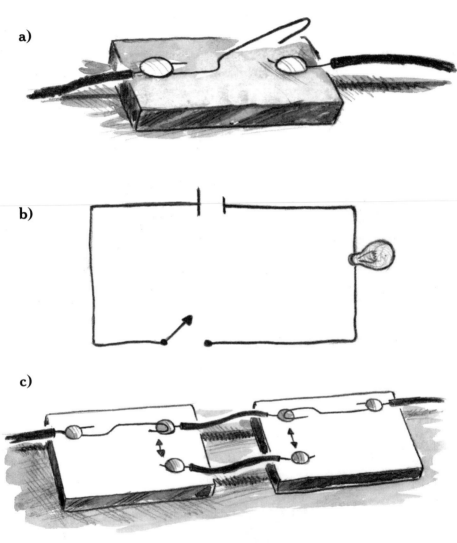

Figure 9.

a) Make a switch using thumbtacks, a paper clip, and a wood block. b) Insert the switch into a circuit. Use it to turn the lightbulb on and off. c) Build a pair of switches that will allow you to turn the bulb on and off at two locations.

If you have a wall switch like those used in your home, insert it into the circuit in place of your paper-clip switch. How should you connect the wires to the switch?

In your home, you can probably find switches that turn a light on from two different locations. For example, a light at the top of a stairway can usually be turned on or off at both the top and bottom of the stairs. To see how such switches work, build a pair of switches like those shown in Figure 9c. In these switches, the paper clips should be flat so they can touch two thumbtacks at the same time. How can you use either switch to turn the light on and off?

Science Project Ideas

- Can you build switches that will allow you to turn a light-bulb on and off from three different locations?

- Ask an electrician to show you how he wires switches that can turn a light on or off from two different places in a building.

Experiment 2.5

Flow of Charge Around a Circuit

Materials

✓ 3 identical bulbs
   (GE #41 or GE #48
   bulbs work well)

✓ 2 D cells

✓ insulated wires

✓ battery holder

✓ 3 bulb sockets

People often think that charge gets used up as it flows around a circuit. However, it is quite easy to show that charge is not used up. All the charge flows all the way around the circuit. To see that this is true, build the circuit shown in Figure 10. It has three identical bulbs wired one after the other and connected to two D cells.

Connect the battery of two D cells to the bulbs. How does the brightness of the three bulbs compare? If charge were used up as it flows around the circuit, how would the brightness of the three bulbs compare? Using a battery of two D cells, how many bulbs can be connected one after the other before the bulbs do not light? If the bulbs do not light, does that mean that no charge is flowing? Or could it be that there is simply not enough charge to make the bulbs glow?

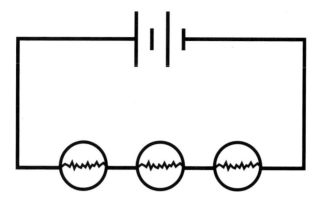

Figure 10.

How does the brightness of three identical bulbs wired in series compare?

Experiment 2.6

Sending Messages Electrically

Materials

- ✓ D cells
- ✓ battery holder
- ✓ flashlight bulbs
- ✓ bulb holders
- ✓ long insulated wires
- ✓ switches from Experiment 2.4
- ✓ a friend

In 1844, Samuel F. B. Morse sent the first long-distance telegraph message over a wire that led from Washington, D.C., to Baltimore, Maryland. He used a code he had invented of dots and dashes. That code, still known as Morse code, is shown in Figure 11. The code also includes periods, commas,

A) • —

B) — • • •

C) — • — •

D) — • •

E) •

F) • • — •

G) — — •

H) • • • •

I) • •

J) • — — —

K) — • —

L) • — • •

M) — —

N) — •

O) — — —

P) • — — •

Q) — — • —

R) • — •

S) • • •

T) —

U) • • —

V) • • • —

W) • — —

X) — • • —

Y) — • — —

Z) — — • •

1) • — — — —

2) • • — — —

3) • • • — —

4) • • • • —

5) • • • • •

6) — • • • •

7) — — • • •

8) — — — • •

9) — — — — •

0) — — — — —

,) — — • • — —

.) • — • — • —

?) • • — — • •

Figure 11.

Morse code consists of dots and dashes that can be made with either light or sound signals.

and question marks, but you may find it more fun to invent your own code for these punctuation marks.

You can use the code, together with an electric circuit, to send messages to a friend in another room. Pressing the switch shown in Figure 12 will cause both the bulb in your room and the bulb

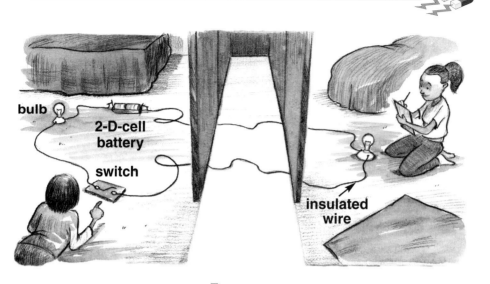

Figure 12.

You can send coded messages using a simple electric circuit.

in the next room to light. Pressing the switch for a short time will produce a dot. Pressing the switch for a longer time will produce a dash.

A similar circuit can be used by your friend to send signals to you.

At first, you will want to keep the code in front of you as you send messages. Later, with practice, you will find that you have learned the code and can send messages more rapidly without looking at the chart.

Science Project Ideas

- Design and build a *single* circuit that will allow both you and your friend to send and receive messages.

- Prepare demonstrations to show how Sir Charles Wheatstone, Samuel Morse, and Joseph Henry were involved in the invention and use of the telegraph.

Experiment 2.7

Short Circuit: The Easy Path

Materials

✓ 2 D cells

✓ battery holder

✓ flashlight bulb

✓ bulb holder

✓ insulated wires

✓ piece of bare (uninsulated) wire

Build a simple circuit like the one shown in Figure 13a. What happens to the flashlight bulb when you touch the ends of a bare (uninsulated) wire to the poles of the D cell as shown in Figure 13b? What happens to the bulb if you use the same bare wire to touch both leads to the bulb as shown in Figure 13c?

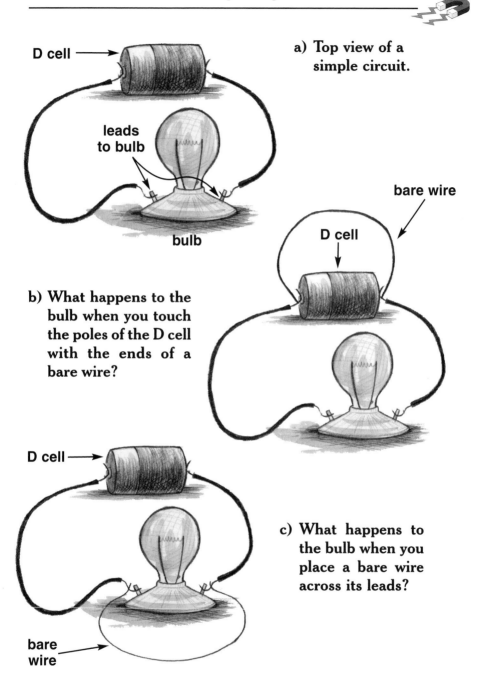

a) Top view of a simple circuit.

D cell

leads to bulb

bulb

bare wire

D cell

b) What happens to the bulb when you touch the poles of the D cell with the ends of a bare wire?

D cell

c) What happens to the bulb when you place a bare wire across its leads?

bare wire

Figure 13.

The bulb lights when electric charges flow from the D cell, through the bulb, and back to the D cell. However, if you provide an alternate path, one that allows charges to flow more easily, the charges will take the easier path. When faced with riding your bike up a steep hill or along a level path, you would probably choose the level path even though it may be a longer ride. It is the easier path for you. Similarly, charges move more easily along a wire, even a long wire, than through a bulb's short filament.

If you have a D cell you can spare, connect the ends of a bare (uninsulated) wire to it. After several minutes, feel the D cell. What do you notice? After an hour, remove the wire and connect the cell to a bulb. How does the brightness of the bulb compare to the brightness of an identical bulb connected to a new D cell?

As you will find, a D cell wears out quickly when its poles are connected to a plain wire. Such a connection creates what is called a short circuit. Because most of the charge flows through the short circuit, there is little charge left to flow through what-ever else may be connected to the cell. When building circuits, be careful not to create short circuits. Your cells will wear out very quickly if you do.

Examine the circuits in Figure 14. In which circuits will the bulb (or bulbs) light? In which are there short circuits? If you are not sure, build the circuit and find out.

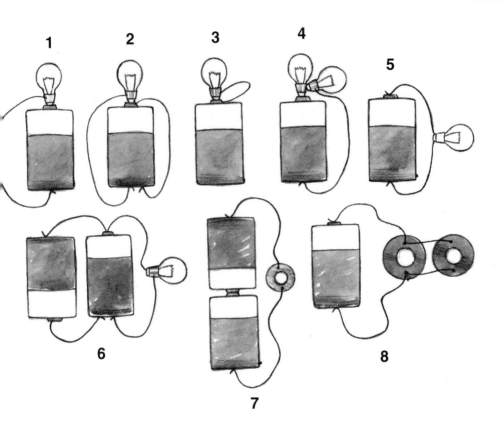

Figure 14.

Which bulbs will light? Where do you find short circuits? Where do you find bulbs that will not light even though there are no short circuits?

Experiment 2.8

Resistors: The Hard Path

Materials

- ✓ insulated wires
- ✓ flashlight bulb
- ✓ bulb socket
- ✓ D cell
- ✓ battery holder
- ✓ thumbtacks

- ✓ 60-cm (24-in) length of #30 (thin) Nichrome wire
- ✓ sheet of cardboard
- ✓ 60-cm (24-in) length of #26 (thick) Nichrome wire

Build the circuit shown in Figure 15a. One insulated wire (wire X) leads from a D cell to a flashlight bulb. The end of a second wire from the D cell (wire Z) is left unconnected. A wire leading from the bulb (wire Y) is also unconnected. Next, connect a 60-cm (24-in) length of thin Nichrome wire between points A and B. Nichrome is a combination of chromium, nickel, and iron commonly used in heating elements. You can run the Nichrome wire back and forth several times around thumbtacks stuck in a sheet of cardboard as shown in Figure 15b. Connect the end of wire Y to one end of the Nichrome wire. Connect the end of wire Z to the other end of the Nichrome wire. By sliding the end of wire Y along the Nichrome wire, you can vary the length of the Nichrome wire between A and B. How does the length

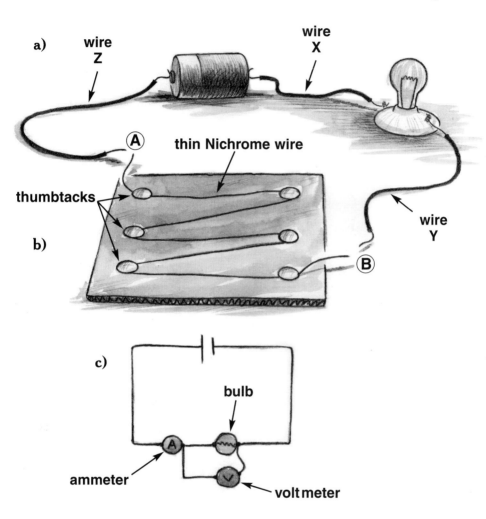

Figure 15.

a) Build the circuit shown here. b) Run a 60-cm- (24-in-) length of Nichrome wire back and forth along a sheet of cardboard. What effect does the Nichrome wire have on the brightness of the bulb? How does the length of the Nichrome wire affect the bulb's brightness? c) Using a voltmeter and an ammeter, you can find the resistance of a lightbulb.

of Nichrome wire between A and B affect the brightness of the bulb?

What does the brightness of the bulb tell you about the amount of charge flowing through the bulb? How does increasing the length of Nichrome wire in the circuit affect the amount of charge flowing around the circuit?

How do you think the results would change if you used a thicker piece of Nichrome wire? Try it! What do you find?

Given equal lengths of Nichrome wire, which offers more resistance to charge flow, the thick or the thin wire?

As you have seen, Nichrome wire, when placed in a circuit, reduces the amount of charge that flows through the circuit. The wire resists the flow of charge because of the elements of which it is made.

The filaments in an incandescent bulb are made of tungsten. Tungsten, too, offers resistance to charge flow. A very high temperature is needed to melt tungsten. Consequently, light-bulb filaments can be heated until they glow with a white light without melting.

Every element in an electric circuit, such as a bulb, a motor, even a D cell, offers some resistance to charge flow. Sometimes elements called resistors are purposely placed in a circuit to reduce the amount of charge flowing through the circuit.

Science Project Ideas

- The resistance of a resistor, lightbulb, or any element in a circuit is defined as the voltage across the element divided by the current through it. Voltage, which is measured in volts, is found by using a voltmeter. Current, which is measured in units called amperes, is found by using an ammeter. An ammeter measures the number of charges per second flowing through a circuit. To measure the resistance of a lightbulb in a circuit, you can build the circuit shown in Figure 15c. As you can see, the ammeter is placed in series with the bulb. The voltmeter is placed in parallel with the bulb.

  Resistance is measured in ohms; one ohm equals one volt per ampere.

  $$1 \text{ ohm} = 1 \text{ volt/ampere}$$

  What is the resistance of the lightbulb according to your measurements?

- Does the resistance of a lightbulb's filament change with temperature? Design and conduct an experiment to find out.

Experiment 2.9

A Burglar Alarm Circuit

Materials

- ✓ piece of cardboard about 15 cm (6 in) by 8 cm (3 in)
- ✓ strips of aluminum foil about 3 cm (1 in) wide
- ✓ long insulated wires with bare ends
- ✓ tape
- ✓ 2-D-cell battery
- ✓ buzzer (buy at an electronics store)
- ✓ carpet or mat

You can build a simple alarm that can be used to detect anyone who enters your house or room. You will need a piece of cardboard about 15 cm (6 in) by 8 cm (3 in). Make a fold line in the cardboard at its center as shown in Figure 16a. Wrap strips of aluminum foil about 3 cm (1 in) wide around the cardboard as shown. Then place the bare ends of two long insulated wires on the aluminum strips. Use tape to fasten the wire to the aluminum strips, and the aluminum to the cardboard. Finish folding the cardboard, being sure the aluminum strips do not touch. Place the folded cardboard under a carpet or mat near a door. Be sure the weight of the carpet does not squeeze the aluminum strips together. Next, connect the wires you taped to the aluminum foil to a 2-D-cell battery and a buzzer, forming the circuit shown in Figure 16b.

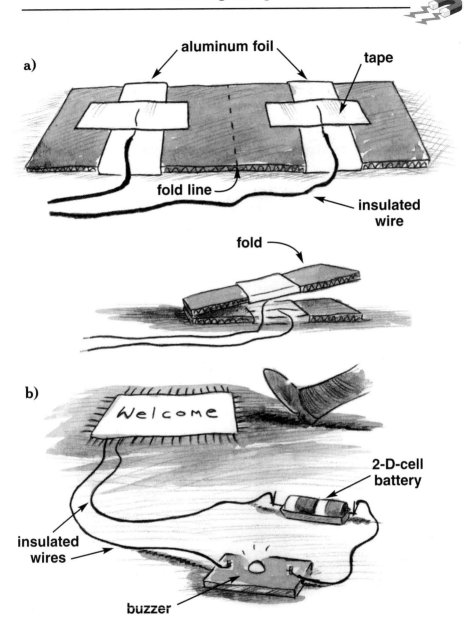

Figure 16.

You can build an alarm that will alert you when people enter your home or room.

When someone steps on the carpet, it will force the aluminum strips together. This will close the circuit and activate the buzzer, letting you know that a person has entered your home or your room.

Experiment 2.10

A Fuse for Safety

Materials

- ✓ clay
- ✓ 3 thick pieces of bare copper wire
- ✓ steel wool
- ✓ 2-D-cell battery
- ✓ insulated wires
- ✓ flashlight bulb and bulb holder

Homes with old electrical wiring may have fuses. In modern homes, fuses have been replaced with circuit breakers. Fuses are widely used in automobile electrical systems and in household appliances. The purpose of a fuse is to prevent a circuit from becoming so hot that it could start a fire.

You can build a circuit with a fuse to see how it works. Use a piece of clay to support two thick pieces of copper wire upright and about half a centimeter apart. Remove a single strand of wire from a pad of steel wool. Wrap the ends of the steel wire firmly around the ends of the two upright copper wires, as shown in Figure 17a. Then build the circuit shown. The thin steel wire will be the fuse in this circuit. When you connect the fuse to

Figure 17.

a) A fuse is connected to a 2-D-cell battery. What will happen?
b) What happens to the fuse when there is a bulb in the circuit? A bulb and a short in the circuit?

the 2-D-cell battery, you will see what happens to a fuse when a large current flows through it.

In a typical circuit, the fuse should not blow. Rebuild the circuit with a flashlight bulb between the battery and the fuse. When you connect this circuit, the fuse should not blow. The bulb's resistance reduces the flow of current. With less charge flowing through the fuse, the fuse does not get hot enough to melt. (If it does melt, use a single D cell rather than two.)

What happens when there is a short circuit? To find out, touch both ends of a short length of bare copper wire to the connections leading to and from the bulb, as shown in Figure 17b. Is the resistance of the copper wire large or small? What happens to the fuse?

Predict what will happen if you rebuild the circuit and connect the bare copper wire to the poles of the battery. Try it! Was your prediction right?

Fuses have to be replaced when they blow. The circuit breakers used in wiring homes today simply have to be reset. Circuit breakers are based on a relationship between electricity and magnetism, which you will explore in the next chapter.

Chapter

Magnets and Magnetic Fields

According to Greek legend, magnets are named for Magnes, a shepherd who noticed that particles of lodestone were attracted to his iron crook. Lodestone, also known as magnetite, is a compound of iron and oxygen that is naturally magnetic. It attracts iron and some other metals. Nearly 5,000 years ago, Chinese observers noticed that narrow chips of magnetite always pointed in the same direction. Their discovery led to the invention of magnetic compasses. Compasses became widely used, especially by sailors on ships far from shore, where there are no landmarks. During cloudy days or nights, when the sun or stars are not visible, a compass enables ships to move in a fixed direction.

You have probably seen a magnetic compass. It is simply a long thin magnet, shaped like an arrow, that rests on a point enclosed in a transparent container. The arrow always points in a northerly direction. However, it does not usually point toward the North Pole. In fact, within the United States, a compass needle may point as much as 20 degrees east or west of the North Pole, which is true north.

Experiment 3.1

Two Magnets

Materials

- ✓ thread
- ✓ tape
- ✓ 2 bar magnets or square or circular ceramic magnets
- ✓ pen and small piece of masking tape (if needed to mark magnets)
- ✓ toothpick
- ✓ magnetic compass
- ✓ drinking straw or stick
- ✓ clay
- ✓ several square or circular ceramic magnets with holes in their centers

Use thread and tape to suspend a bar magnet or a square or circular ceramic magnet. If you use a small square or circular magnet, tape a toothpick to the magnet as shown in Figure 18. Notice that once the magnet stops turning, it always points in a northerly direction. If it does not point in a northerly

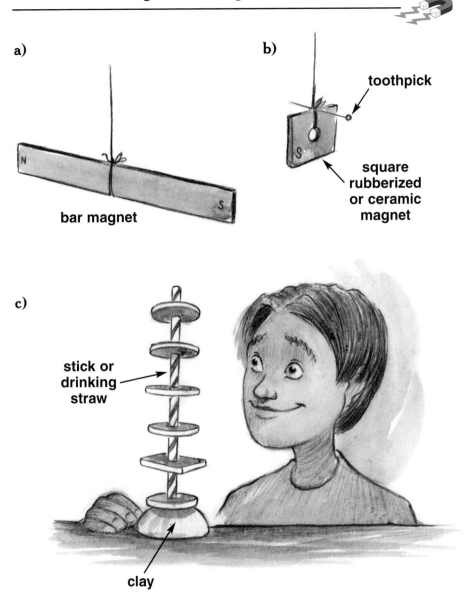

a)

bar magnet

b)

toothpick

square
rubberized
or ceramic
magnet

c)

stick or
drinking
straw

clay

Figure 18.

Suspend a bar magnet (a) or a square or round ceramic magnet
(b) by a thread. Notice that the magnet always points in
the same direction. c) Can you make a set of floating magnets
like these?

direction, there are other magnetic materials nearby. Move the experiment to a point far from any metallic material.

Once the suspended magnet is at rest, mark the end or side that is northernmost with an *N* if it is not already marked. Mark the other end or side with an *S*. Repeat the process with a second magnet. Again, if not already marked, mark the northernmost side or end with an *N* and the southernmost end or side with an *S*. The ends or sides of the magnets that you have marked N or S are called poles. The pole marked N is the north-seeking pole of the magnet. The pole marked S is the south-seeking pole.

What happens when you bring the north-seeking pole of one magnet near the north-seeking pole of a second magnet?

What happens when you bring the north-seeking pole of one magnet near the south-seeking pole of a second magnet?

Predict what will happen when you bring the south-seeking pole of one magnet near the south-seeking pole of a second magnet. Try it! Was your prediction correct?

What can you conclude about the force between like poles of two magnets? What can you conclude about the force between opposite (N and S) poles of two magnets?

What do you think will happen if you slowly bring the north-seeking pole of a magnet near the north-seeking pole of a compass needle? Try it! Were you right?

What do you think will happen if you slowly bring the south-seeking pole of a magnet near the north-seeking pole of a compass needle?

Obtain several square or circular ceramic magnets with holes in their centers. Figure out a way to place these magnets on a drinking straw or stick so that they float like the ones shown in Figure 18c.

Science Project Ideas

● You can turn a nail into a magnet. Hold the nail against a piece of wood with one hand. Use the other hand to stroke the entire length of the nail with a bar magnet. Apply all strokes in the same direction and with the same pole of the magnet. After about 30 strokes, test the nail to see if it behaves like a magnet. If it does, how does its polarity compare with the pole you used to stroke the nail?

● Having made a magnet, investigate ways to remove its magnetic properties.

● To make a simple compass, like ones used by ancient sailors, turn a sewing needle into a magnet by stroking it with a bar magnet. Remove the bottom from a Styrofoam cup and put it in a bowl of water. Place the needle on the Styrofoam disk. Does the needle behave like a magnetic compass?

● Use your ingenuity to make a variety of magnetic compasses from ordinary materials you can find in your home or school.

EARTH AS A MAGNET

The fact that a compass needle points in a northerly direction suggests that Earth behaves like a giant magnet, as shown in Figure 19. Suppose you were to take a compass to the Boothia Peninsula, north of Hudson Bay, in northern Canada, about 1,200 miles from Earth's geographic North Pole. There, at about 76 degrees latitude, 100 degrees west longitude, you would find the compass needle points straight down, indicating it is over one of Earth's magnetic poles. But think! If the north-seeking pole of your compass points downward at this pole, is Earth's magnetic pole under Boothia Peninsula a north-seeking or a south-seeking pole?

Similarly, suppose you took a compass to a point in Antarctica near Dumont d'Urville, about 1,200 miles from Earth's geographic South Pole. There, at about 67 degrees latitude, 140 degrees east longitude, you would find the compass needle's north-seeking pole pointing straight up. Is Earth's magnetic pole in Antarctica a north-seeking or a south-seeking pole?

Since Earth's magnetic poles are not located at its north and south geographic poles, compass needles seldom point toward true north. Within half a degree, the North Star is directly above our North Pole. At night, a compass needle is not likely to point in the direction of the North Star. For example, a compass near Boston, Massachusetts, will point about 15 degrees west of true

Earth's North Pole

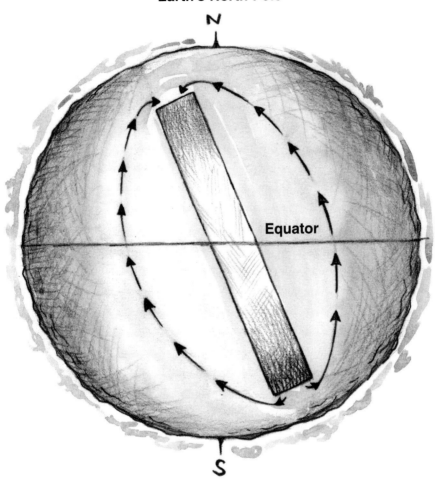

Earth's South Pole

Figure 19.

Earth behaves as if it contained a giant magnet. The small arrows show the general direction of compass needles at various points on Earth's surface. At a point in the northern hemisphere, above one of Earth's magnetic poles, a compass needle will point straight down toward the ground.

geographic north. A compass near San Diego, California, will point about 15 degrees east of true geographic north. But there are points where a compass needle does point toward true north. Such a region lies along the Georgia-South Carolina border.

The difference between true geographic north and magnetic north is called the magnetic declination. However, Earth's magnetism is constantly changing. Therefore, charts showing the angles of magnetic declination on Earth's surface have to be revised frequently.

Around every magnet, including whatever acts like a magnet inside Earth, there is a magnetic field. We cannot see the field, but it can be mapped and its force revealed by compass needles. You will map a magnetic field in the next experiment.

A Magnetic Field

Materials

- ✓ 2 bar magnets
- ✓ sheets of white paper
- ✓ pencil
- ✓ magnetic compass
- ✓ iron filings
- ✓ scissors (optional)

- ✓ steel wool (optional)
- ✓ old salt or pepper shaker (optional)
- ✓ tape
- ✓ thin sheet of cardboard

In the early 1800s, Michael Faraday, an English scientist, experimented with electricity and magnetism. He found it useful to think of magnets as if they were surrounded by lines of force. If a compass needle is placed near a magnet, it will point in a particular direction. To Faraday, the compass needle near a magnet revealed the direction of the line of force at the location of the compass. The magnetic field around the magnet consisted of all the lines of force.

You can map the lines of force around a bar magnet. Place the magnet on a sheet of white paper. Use a pencil to mark the direction a compass needle points as the compass is moved around the magnet (see Figure 20a). The direction of a magnetic field at any point is defined as the direction given by the north-seeking end of a compass needle. Begin with the compass near the south pole of the magnet. Simply move the compass to an adjacent position in the direction the compass needle was pointing. Repeat this process until you reach the magnet's north pole.

You could repeat this a number of times to obtain the entire field around the magnet. However, there is an easier way to reveal the field around a magnet. Iron filings, small pieces of iron, behave like tiny compass needles. You can probably obtain iron filings from a science teacher or a hobby shop. If not, you can make your own. Over a sheet of paper, use scissors to cut part of a roll of steel wool into tiny pieces. Use the paper to pour the particles into an old salt or pepper shaker.

Once you have some iron filings, tape a sheet of white paper to a thin sheet of cardboard. Place the cardboard on top of a bar magnet. Then sprinkle some iron filings over the paper. Tap the cardboard gently. The filings will align themselves like tiny compass needles, revealing the field lines about the bar magnet. Does the field resemble the one shown in Figure 20b?

To see the pattern near repelling magnetic poles, tape two bar magnets in place with their north-seeking poles about 5 cm (2 in) apart (see Figure 20c). Use paper, cardboard, and iron filings to examine the magnetic field pattern near repelling poles.

Repeat the experiment to find the magnetic field pattern between attracting magnetic poles.

Because a compass needle on Earth points in a particular direction, we know there is a magnetic field above Earth. The

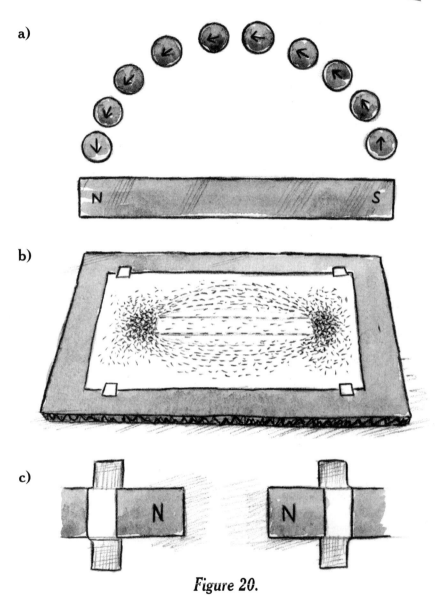

Figure 20.

a) A small compass can be used to map lines of force (field lines) around a bar magnet. b) A magnetic field is revealed by iron filings. c) What does the field near repelling poles look like?

pattern of this field is similar to the field you found around a bar magnet. Suppose you were to follow one of Earth's magnetic field lines as indicated by a compass needle. Where would your journey take you?

Science Project Ideas

- Design and carry out an experiment to find out whether or not the tiny particles in an iron-enriched cereal will respond to a magnet.

- Prepare a mixture of iron filings, salt, and sawdust. Design an experiment to separate the three components of the mixture.

- Which part of a bar magnet is stronger, the poles or the middle? Design and conduct an experiment to find out.

- Place two bar magnets in a line about 10 cm (4 in) apart with their north poles facing each other. Place a small compass between the poles. Find a point at which the compass needle is not turned toward either pole. (The needle is at a right angle to an imaginary line connecting the two poles.) Why does such a point between repelling poles exist? Is there a similar point for poles that attract?

- How can you use waxed paper and iron filings to prepare permanent magnetic field patterns?

Experiment 3.3

Magnets, Magnetic Matter, and Nonmagnetic Matter

Materials

✓ tape

✓ thread

✓ 2 magnets

✓ magnetic compass

✓ piece of wood

✓ small test tube

✓ iron filings

✓ paper clip

✓ a cork

✓ a variety of objects such as steel, copper, or aluminum nails, brass screws or tacks, cardboard, tin, aluminum cans, wooden pencils, etc.

You have seen that a magnet has two poles (N and S). You have also demonstrated that like poles (N-N or S-S) repel and unlike poles (N-S) attract. You can use what you know to classify various materials into three groups: magnets, magnetic matter, and nonmagnetic matter. A magnet will both attract and repel another magnet. Magnetic matter can be magnetized. Such matter is attracted by a magnet but is not a magnet itself. Once the attracting magnet is removed, the matter will not behave like a magnet. Finally, nonmagnetic matter is not affected by a magnet. It is neither attracted nor repelled by a magnet.

To begin, use tape and thread to suspend a magnet. Then bring a variety of objects near the magnet. You might try such things as another magnet; nails made of steel, copper, or aluminum; plastic; glass; brass screws or tacks; cardboard; paper; tin cans (actually steel coated with tin); aluminum cans; plastic wrap; aluminum foil; paper; wax paper; brass; rubber bands or erasers; wooden pencils; plastic rulers; paper clip; thumbtack; and whatever else you can find.

Which of the materials attracted the magnet? Did any repel the magnet? If something attracted the magnet, did you turn it around to see if it would repel the magnet?

Classify the materials you tested into things that are magnets, magnetic matter, and nonmagnetic matter.

Sometimes magnetic matter can be made into a magnet. For example, hold a paper clip near a magnetic compass. The paper clip should have no effect on the compass needle. If it does, choose another paper clip. Next, hold the paper clip against a piece of wood. Then stroke the entire length of the paper clip with a bar magnet. Apply all strokes in the same direction and with the same pole of the magnet. After about 30 strokes, bring the paper clip near a magnetic compass. Does one end of the paper clip act like a south-seeking pole, while the other end acts like a north-seeking pole?

Fill a small test tube with iron filings. Put a cork in the tube so that the filings cannot fall out. Again, stroke the entire length of the test tube with a bar magnet as you did the paper clip. Carefully pick up the test tube in a horizontal position. Bring the test tube close to a magnetic compass. Has the test tube of filings become a magnet? If it has, which end is the north pole? The south pole?

Carefully put the test tube aside for use in the next experiment.

Experiment 3.4

Unmaking a Magnet

Materials

✓ **an adult**

✓ small test tube with iron filings from Experiment 3.3

✓ magnetic compass

✓ paper clips

✓ a strong magnet

✓ thread

✓ hard floor

✓ hammer

✓ pliers

✓ candle

✓ matches

As you have seen, a magnet can be made by stroking a piece of iron or steel with a strong magnet. The reason this works is that the atoms of certain elements such as iron each behave like tiny magnets. In an unmagnetized piece of iron, the atoms are arranged in a random fashion. As a result, the tiny magnets cancel one another's magnetism, as shown in Figure 21a. When the iron is properly stroked with a magnet, the atoms are forced to line up with more of their poles pointing in one direction than any other, as shown in Figure 21b.

Most magnets are made of steel or an alloy of nickel, cobalt, aluminum, and iron. Ceramic magnets are made by embedding oxides of iron, nickel, and beryllium in clay. These magnets are called permanent magnets because they retain their magnetism.

Are there ways to demagnetize magnets? You might guess that jarring the atoms from their alignment would destroy their magnetism. Perhaps dropping the magnets would demagnetize them or at least reduce their strength.

To test this idea, hold the small test tube of iron filings from Experiment 3.3 and thoroughly shake it several times. Then bring the test tube close to a magnetic compass. Has the tube of filings lost all or most of its magnetism?

To further test this idea, magnetize two paper clips by stroking each of them with a strong magnet as you did in

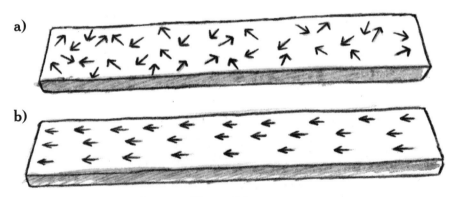

Figure 21.

a) The magnetic atoms in an unmagnetized piece of iron are arranged in a random manner. As a result their magnetic effects cancel one another. b) When magnetized, the poles of the atoms are aligned, creating a strong magnetic field.

Experiment 3.3. Suspend one of the paper-clip magnets from a thread. Bring one pole of the second paper-clip magnet near a pole of the suspended magnet. Do the two poles attract or repel? Use the two paper-clip magnets to show that like poles repel and unlike poles attract.

Next, drop both magnetized paper clips on a hard floor several times. Again suspend one paper clip from a thread and bring the second paper clip near the suspended one. Has dropping the paper-clip magnets eliminated or reduced their magnetism?

Will hammering magnetized paper clips also demagnetize them? Carry out an experiment to find out.

When solid substances are heated, their atoms or molecules vibrate more rapidly. Perhaps heating could also cause the atoms in a magnetic material to be jarred out of alignment. This would eliminate or reduce their magnetism.

To test this idea, again magnetize two paper clips by stroking them with a strong magnet. Check, as before, to be sure the paper clips have been magnetized. Then **ask an adult** to heat each paper clip by using pliers to hold each paper clip in a candle flame for a few seconds.

After the paper clips have cooled, suspend one paper clip from a thread and bring the second paper clip near the suspended one. Has heating the paper-clip magnets eliminated or reduced their magnetism?

Experiment 3.5

Can a Magnetic Field Act Through Materials?

Materials

- ✓ bar magnet
- ✓ books
- ✓ table
- ✓ thread
- ✓ paper clip
- ✓ tape

- ✓ various materials such as cardboard, paper, plastic, aluminum foil, a tin can lid, glass, a saucer, water-filled saucer, a cookie tin, and coins
- ✓ scissors

You know that a magnetic field can attract or repel magnets or magnetic matter through air. Can such a field act through other kinds of matter?

To find out, place a bar magnet under the top book in a stack of books resting on a table, as shown in Figure 22. Tie one end of a piece of thread to a paper clip. Tape the other end to the table. The magnet should be strong enough to keep the paper clip suspended, as shown in the drawing.

With the magnetic field keeping the paper clip floating below the magnet, place different samples of thin materials between the magnet and the paper clip. You might try pieces of cardboard, paper, plastic, aluminum foil, a tin can lid, glass, a saucer, a water-filled saucer, a cookie tin, and coins.

Figure 22.

Can a magnetic field act through materials other than air?

Through which materials, if any, can the magnetic field pass? Which materials, if any, block the magnetic field? Do you think you can "cut" the field with scissors? Try it! Were you right?

Chapter 4

Magnetism From Electricity

As you have seen, electricity and magnetism have much in common. In the case of electricity, like charges (+ and + or – and –) repel one another, and unlike charges (+ and –) attract one another. In the case of magnets, like poles (N and N or S and S) repel one another, and opposite poles (N and S) attract one another. Furthermore, both electric and magnetic forces can be exerted through space; the charges or poles do not have to touch for their effects to be observed.

Because of their similarities, many scientists thought that electricity and magnetism were related. However, until 1819, no one could find a connection between them. That year, Hans

Christian Oersted, a Danish physicist, accidentally discovered the connecting link when he brought a magnetic compass near a current-carrying wire. Experiment 4.1 will lead you to the same discovery that Oersted made nearly 200 years ago.

Experiment 4.1

Oersted's Discovery

Materials

✓ magnetic compass
✓ table or counter
✓ D cell

✓ long insulated wire
with bare ends

Place a magnetic compass on a table or counter. Lay a long insulated wire on top of the compass. The wire should be parallel to the compass needle, as shown in Figure 23. Connect one bared end of the long wire to the pole of a D cell. Briefly touch the other bared end of the wire to the other pole of the D cell. What happens to the compass needle?

Connect the D cell to the wire again and keep current flowing until you can determine the direction the compass needle is pointing. (Do not leave the circuit connected any longer than necessary. The D cell will wear out quickly if it generates a large current.)

Based on this experiment, what is one connection between electricity and magnetism?

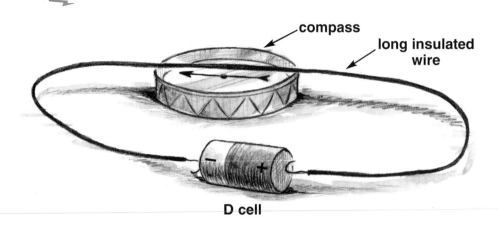

compass

long insulated wire

D cell

Figure 23.

What did Oersted discover about the link between electricity and magnetism?

Next, put the wire *under* the compass and repeat the experiment. What happens this time? Is anything different?

Leave the wire under the compass and turn the D cell around so that current will flow in the opposite direction. What do you observe this time when charge flows through the wire?

Science Project Idea

- In Experiment 3.5, you found that a magnetic field can exert its effects through some kinds of matter such as paper and plastic. Can the magnetic field created by an electric current exert its effect through similar materials? Design an experiment to find out.

Experiment 4.2

An Electric Current's Magnetic Field

Materials

✓ long, straight piece of heavy copper wire

✓ cardboard box

✓ 4 D cells or 6-volt dry cell battery

✓ battery holder(s)

✓ insulated wires

✓ 1 or more magnetic compasses

✓ a partner

As you saw in the previous experiment, an electric current produces a magnetic field. But what does the magnetic field around a current look like? What is its direction? Does it resemble the field around a bar magnet?

To find out, push a long, straight piece of heavy copper wire through one side of a cardboard box, as shown in Figure 24a. Construct a battery consisting of 4 D cells connected end to end, or use a 6-volt dry cell battery. Attach insulated wires to the battery as shown. Briefly connect the ends of the insulated wires to the copper wire. Of course, this is a short circuit, so **it should not be connected for more than a few seconds**. If you have six or more magnetic compasses, place them around the wire as shown. If you only have one compass, have a partner move the compass around the wire while you watch.

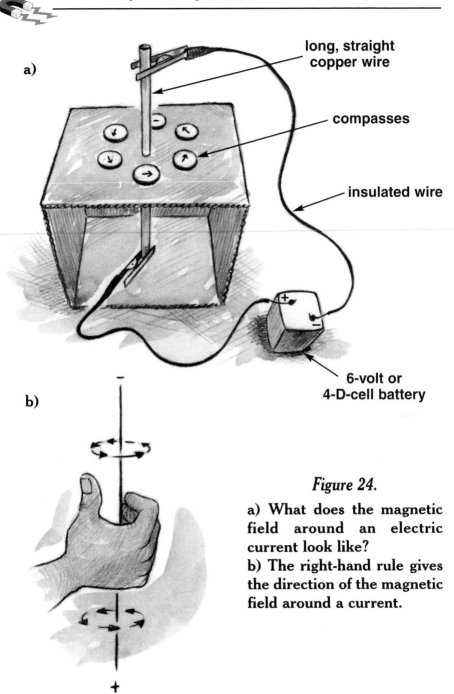

a)

long, straight
copper wire

compasses

insulated wire

6-volt or
4-D-cell battery

b)

Figure 24.

a) **What does the magnetic field around an electric current look like?**
b) **The right-hand rule gives the direction of the magnetic field around a current.**

As you will see, the magnetic field lines form a circular pattern around the electric current that flows in the wire. The direction of the field lines can be predicted by what is known as the right-hand rule. Point your thumb in the direction that positive charge would flow through the wire. Assume positive charge flows from the battery's positive pole to its negative pole. Your fingers curl in the direction of the magnetic field around the wire. Remember, the direction of a magnetic field is given by the direction the north-seeking pole of a compass needle points. (See Figure 24b.) Do your results agree with this rule?

Science Project Ideas

- Repeat Experiment 4.2 using iron filings in place of compass needles. What do iron filings reveal more clearly about the pattern? What don't they reveal?

- Based on what you have learned about magnetic fields in Experiments 4.1 and 4.2, how can you explain the existence of Earth's magnetic field?

Experiment 4.3

An Electric Meter

Materials

✓ **an adult**

✓ 10 m (33 ft) of 24-gauge insulated wire

✓ roll of duct tape

✓ knife or wire stripper

✓ tape

✓ clay or tape

✓ cardboard

✓ scissors

✓ magnetic compass

✓ insulated wires

✓ D cell

Since an electric current creates a magnetic field that surrounds the current, it can turn a compass needle, as you have seen. The interaction between an electric current and a magnet can serve as the basis of a meter that can detect electric currents.

To make a simple meter, wind about 10 m (33 ft) of 24-gauge insulated wire around a roll of duct tape to make a coil, as shown in Figure 25a. Use some tape to keep the coils in place. Leave about 30 cm (1 ft) of wire at each end of the coil. **Ask an adult** to use a knife or wire stripper to remove about 4 cm (1.5 in) of insulation from each end of the wire. Use clay or tape to support the coil upright as shown.

Fold a strip of cardboard to form a platform that will support a compass at the center of the coil. The compass needle should be aligned with (parallel to) the plane of the coils. Use insulated wires to connect the coil to a D cell.

a)

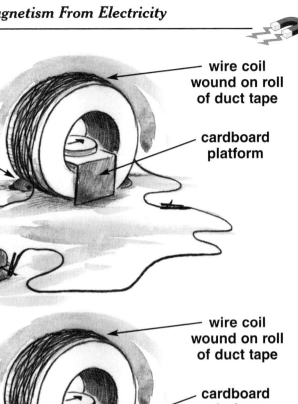

wire coil
wound on roll
of duct tape

cardboard
platform

clay

D cell

b)

wire coil
wound on roll
of duct tape

cardboard
platform

clay

D cell

objects being tested

c)

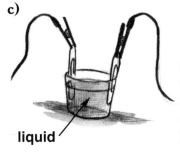

liquid

Figure 25.

a) You can make a simple meter that can detect an electric current. The meter can be used to test the ability of different materials, (b) solids (c) liquids, to conduct charges.

What happens to the compass needle when current flows through the coil? Let the current flow just long enough so that you can see the direction of the magnetic field at the center of the coil. Is this the direction you would expect from the right-hand rule?

Turn the D cell around so that current will flow in the opposite direction. Predict the direction of the magnetic field at the coil's center after making this change. Was your prediction right?

Experiment 4.4

Using an Electric Meter to Test for Conductivity

Materials

- ✓ insulated wires
- ✓ meter from Experiment 4.3
- ✓ solid objects such as cardboard, nails, plastic, pencils, pencil lead, silverware, wood, paper, coins, candle wax, chalk, glass, rubber bands, paper clips, aluminum foil, and flashlight bulb
- ✓ 4 D cells
- ✓ small plastic medicine cup or vial
- ✓ paper clips
- ✓ liquids such as water, milk, lemon and other juices, vinegar, carbonated soda, and solutions of salt, sugar, and baking soda

You can use the simple electric meter you built in the previous experiment to find out which materials conduct charge and which do not. To do this, build the circuit shown in Figure 25b. Connect an insulated wire to each end of the D cell. One of these wires should be connected to one end of the coil. The second will be used to touch one side of the object to be tested. Connect a third wire to the other end of the coil; it will be used to touch the other side of the object being tested.

Solid objects you might test could include cardboard, nails, plastic, pencils, pencil lead, silverware, wood, paper, coins, candle wax, chalk, glass, rubber bands, paper clips, aluminum foil, or a flashlight bulb.

To test these solids, touch the ends of the object you are testing with the ends of the two wires, one from the D cell and one from the coil. (**Do not touch for more than a second or two; a large current wears out D cells quickly.**) If the meter's compass needle turns, you know that the material is conducting charge. What will you observe if the item does not conduct charge?

Which materials are conductors? Which appear to be nonconductors?

From your tests, can you explain why rubber bands were suggested for making battery holders in Experiment 2.2? What would happen if the rubber bands were replaced by metal straps? Why were paper clips used to make contact with the poles of the battery? Could you have used cardboard strips instead?

Test the various parts of a flashlight bulb. Is the metal side of the bulb a conductor? How about the small metal knob at the bottom of the bulb? What about the ceramic material around the metal knob? How do you know that the bulb's filament is a conductor? Can you explain now why the wires have to touch certain places to make a bulb light?

Charge must flow through the inside of a D cell, but which parts of the outside of a D cell will conduct charge?

Do you think any liquids will conduct electric charge? To find out, place the liquid you want to test in a small plastic medicine cup or vial. Slide two paper clips over the sides of the container as shown in Figure 25c. The lower half of each clip should be submerged in liquid. Touch the lead wire from the D cell to the top of one paper clip. Check to be sure that the two paper clips are not in contact, then touch the other paper clip with the wire from the coil.

Test a number of different liquids such as water, milk, lemon and other juices, vinegar, carbonated soda, and solutions of salt, sugar, and baking soda. If the meter needle turns, what does this tell you about the liquid you are testing?

If the meter's needle does not turn, the liquid may be a nonconductor, or it may be a poor conductor. Do you see gas bubbles forming around either of the paper clips? The bubbles show that even though there is not enough electric current to turn the needle, there is enough to cause some kind of chemical reaction around the paper clips. Will the needle turn if you use a 2-D-cell battery? A 4-D-cell battery?

Experiment 4.5

Magnetic Coils

Materials

- ✓ Two 5-m (16-ft) lengths of 24-gauge enamel-coated copper wire
- ✓ 2 D cells
- ✓ tape
- ✓ fine sandpaper
- ✓ insulated wires with alligator clips
- ✓ paper clips
- ✓ magnetic compass

Once Oersted's discovery became known, scientists realized that magnets could be made by sending electric currents through coils of wire. André Ampère, a French physicist, showed that the magnetic effects produced by electricity could be used to detect and measure electric current. You have already built a coil that can detect a current. In this experiment, you will see that current-carrying coils really do behave like magnets.

Obtain two 5-m (16-ft) lengths of 24-gauge enamel-coated copper wire. (The enamel on the wire insulates it so that you can wind the wire into a coil without producing a short circuit.) Wind each length of wire into a coil by wrapping it around a

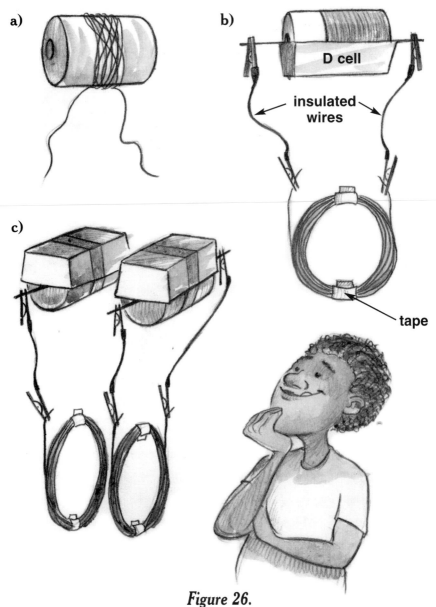

Figure 26.

a) Make two coils by winding enamel-coated wire around a D cell. b) Suspend the coils from a D cell. Are the coils magnetic? c) Bring two coils close together. What happens?

D cell as shown in Figure 26a. Slide the coil of wire off the D cell. Wrap small pieces of tape around the coils to hold the wires in place. Leave about 30 cm (1 ft) of wire uncoiled at each end. These straight wires will be used to connect the coil to a D cell. Use fine sandpaper to remove about 3 cm (1 in) of enamel insulation from each end of each coil.

If you attach the two ends of the wire from a coil to a D cell as shown in Figure 26b, a current will flow through the coil. **Do not leave the coil connected longer than necessary or you will wear out the D cell!** With the coil hanging from a D cell, bring a magnetic compass close to the coil. How can you tell that the coil behaves like a magnet? Which side of the coil is the north-seeking pole?

Attach the second coil to another D cell. Does it also behave like a magnet? What do you think will happen if you hold the faces of these two coils close together, as shown in Figure 26c? Try it! Were you right? How can you make the coils repel one another? How can you make them attract one another?

Experiment 4.6

Electromagnets

Materials

✓ 1 meter (1 yard) of enamel-coated copper wire

✓ iron nail

✓ sandpaper

✓ D cell

✓ paper clips

Oersted's discovery of the magnetic field around moving charge led almost immediately to new technology. William Sturgeon, an English physicist, accidentally discovered that if a coil of wire were wrapped around an iron core, the strength of the magnetic field would be concentrated in the iron. He used varnish on a U-shaped piece of iron to insulate it from the metal wire. He then ran a current through the wire coil and was able to lift a 4-kg (9-lb) weight with an iron core that weighed only 0.2 kg (7 oz).

A short time later, American physicist Joseph Henry improved upon Sturgeon's design. He wrapped silk strips torn from his wife's old dresses to insulate wire he wound around an iron core. By so doing he was able to wind layer after layer of wire around the iron. In 1831, at a demonstration at Yale University, Henry lifted more than a ton of iron with what became known as an electromagnet.

Today, this technology is used to lift and move huge piles of scrap metal. First the scrap metal is lifted with an electromagnet. The scrap metal is moved. Then the current in the coil is reversed. This changes the polarity of the electromagnet. Since the magnetism that was induced in the scrap metal was of the opposite magnetic polarity, it is no longer attracted by the electromagnet and falls off. Electromagnets are also used to seal bank vaults.

To make a small electromagnet, wrap about a meter (a yard) of enamel-coated copper wire around an iron nail. Always wrap the wire in the same direction. Sandpaper the ends of the wire to remove the enamel. Connect the ends of the coil to a D cell, as shown in Figure 27.

How many paper clips can your electromagnet lift? (Do not connect the electromagnet to the battery for very long. The battery will wear out quickly under such conditions.)

How many paper clips can you lift with the coil if you take out the nail?

Rebuild the electromagnet, but this time wind half the turns in one direction and the other half in the opposite direction. Predict the number of paper clips your electromagnet will lift now. Were you right? Can you explain why?

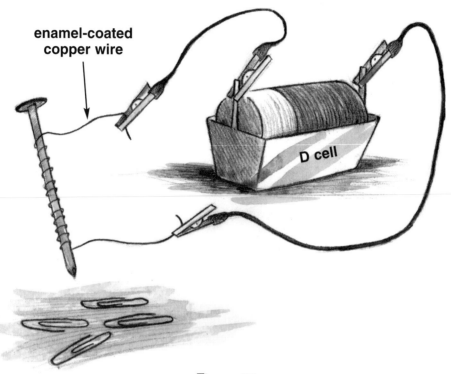

Figure 27.

You can make an electromagnet. How strong is it?

Science Project Ideas

- Design an experiment to show whether the number of turns in the coil affects the strength of an electromagnet.

- Can metals other than iron or steel be used as the cores for an electromagnet? Design an experiment to find out.

Chapter

Electricity, Magnets, and Motors

fter Oersted discovered that magnetic fields are produced by electric currents, scientists began to look for other connections between electricity and magnetism. Within a year of Oersted's discovery, the great English scientist Michael Faraday made another scientific breakthrough. Faraday reasoned that if a current could produce a force on a magnet, a magnet should be able to produce a force on a current. In Experiment 5.1, you will perform an experiment similar to one that Faraday, in England, and Joseph Henry, in the United States, conducted to test this idea.

Faraday and Henry also reasoned that since moving charge can produce a magnetic field, a magnetic field should be able to make charges move. That is, it should be possible to use a magnetic field to induce an electric current in a wire. In Experiment 5.3, you will find, as did Faraday and Henry, the secret to using a magnetic field to induce an electric current.

Experiment 5.1

A Current in a Magnetic Field

Materials

- ✓ strong horseshoe magnet or 4 to 6 ceramic magnets
- ✓ bare copper wire
- ✓ D cell
- ✓ insulated wires
- ✓ tape

You have seen that a magnetic field surrounds an electric current. When charges move, a magnetic field is created. Will a magnetic field have any effect on an electric current? You might think so. After all, an electric current is surrounded by a magnetic field, and magnetic fields can attract or repel one another.

To find out, you can use either a strong horseshoe magnet or four to six ceramic magnets. If you use a horseshoe magnet, suspend a swing-shaped piece of bare copper wire from a D cell as shown in Figure 28a. Use insulated wires to connect the

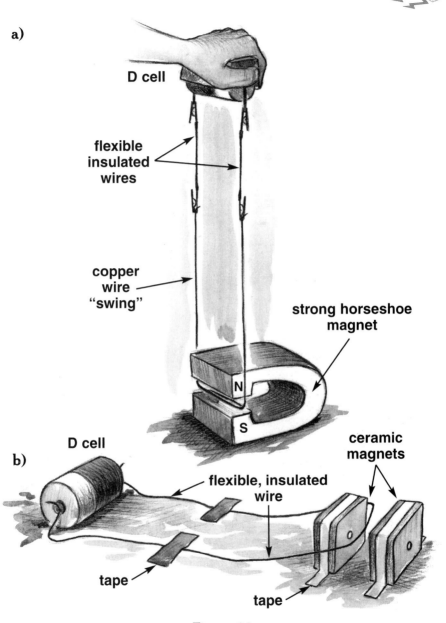

a)

D cell

flexible
insulated
wires

copper
wire
"swing"

strong horseshoe
magnet

N

S

D cell

ceramic
magnets

b)

flexible, insulated
wire

tape

tape

Figure 28.

To see the effect of a magnetic field on a current, let a current
flow in a direction perpendicular to a magnetic field.

copper wire to the D cell. Be sure the suspended copper wire can swing freely. Bring the short side of the copper wire between the poles of the magnet as shown. Then connect the wire to a D cell so that a current flows through the copper wire in the magnetic field. The wire will be pushed either into or out of the magnet. Which way is it pushed? What happens to the direction the wire is pushed if you turn the D cell around?

If you use ceramic magnets, place four or six of the magnets so that they are attracted to each other and form a column. Divide the group of magnets in the middle so that you have two groups of magnets. The two groups will attract one another. Separate the two groups by 1 cm (0.5 in) and tape them down that far apart.

Use a long, flexible, insulated wire to make a loop as shown in Figure 28b. The ends of the wire should be bare. Place the loop—the center of the wire—between the faces of the magnets. Tape the wire in place as shown. Be sure the loop between the magnets can move up or down easily. Then touch the bare ends of the wire to the opposite poles of a D cell. Notice that the loop of wire between the faces of the magnets is pushed either up or down. Which way is it pushed? What happens to the direction the wire is pushed if you turn the D cell around? How might this basic principle be used to build an electric motor?

Science Project Idea

● Design and carry out an experiment to measure the force exerted on a current by a magnetic field. Does the size of the force depend on the current? Does the size of the force depend on the strength of the magnetic field?

ELECTRIC MOTORS

Faraday discovered that there is a force on a current-carrying wire when the current runs across a magnetic field. He realized that such a force could be used to make a motor that would do work. He demonstrated that possibility by building the simple motor shown in Figure 29.

Today, electric motors are everywhere, and, in increasing numbers, they are found in automobiles. Gasoline-powered cars contribute to air pollution and produce greenhouse gases, such as carbon dioxide, that cause global warming. Electric cars powered by fuel cells do not. Replacing gasoline-powered cars with electric cars would reduce pollution and greenhouse gases significantly.

A variety of electric cars are on the market or being developed. All of them have an efficient motor that turns the car's wheels and obtains and stores energy when the car slows down. The energy obtained during slowdowns (braking) returns as

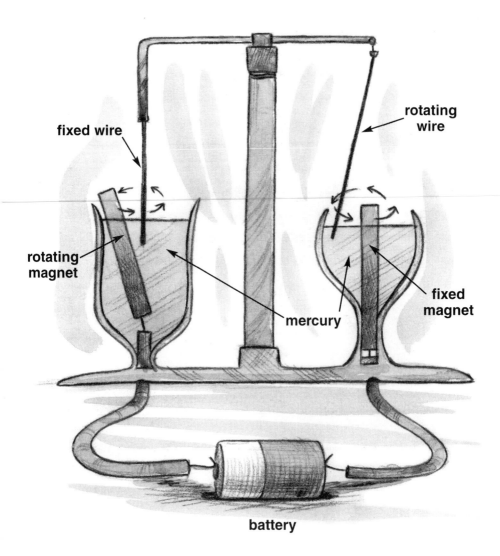

Figure 29.

In Faraday's electric motor, a magnet rotated around a fixed wire (left), and a wire rotated around a fixed magnet (right). A battery provided current, and mercury allowed current to reach both the fixed and the rotating wires.

much as half of the car's kinetic (motion) energy to batteries or fuel cells. Furthermore, unlike an internal combustion engine, the electric motor requires no energy when at rest or coasting. A gasoline engine makes use of less than one fourth of the energy in the fuel it burns. On the other hand, an electric motor can change more than 90 percent of the potential energy stored in the chemicals of the battery that drive it into kinetic energy. Electric cars powered by hydrogen fuel cells release only water as an end product. Gone are the carbon monoxide and carbon dioxide gases that contribute to pollution and global warming.

Increasingly popular are hybrid cars. These cars are powered by an electric motor combined with a small internal combustion engine. The internal combustion engine is used to charge batteries or fuel cells when necessary. The drawback to electric or hybrid cars is their initial cost. However, fuel costs are considerably less, and electric motors have a longer life span. When the health and economic costs related to pollution and global warming are considered, electric cars are very competitive.

Experiment 5.2

A Current in a Magnetic Field and Motors

Materials

- ✓ **an adult**
- ✓ Styrofoam cup
- ✓ 2 large paper clips
- ✓ tape
- ✓ 3 ceramic magnets
- ✓ 30-cm (1-ft) length of enamel-coated copper wire
- ✓ sandpaper
- ✓ insulated wires with alligator clips
- ✓ 4-D-cell battery or 6-volt dry cell battery
- ✓ pliers
- ✓ plastic darning or thin knitting needle
- ✓ wine cork
- ✓ sharp knife

- ✓ about 8 m (25 ft) of thin enamel-coated copper wire
- ✓ pins
- ✓ tin snips
- ✓ tin can
- ✓ hammer
- ✓ small nail
- ✓ wood block about 15 cm x 15 cm x 2.5 cm (6 in x 6 in x 1 in)
- ✓ 3 tacks or small screws
- ✓ two 30-cm (1-ft) pieces of insulated copper wire
- ✓ thumbtacks
- ✓ strong horseshoe magnet or 6 to 8 ceramic magnets

You have seen that a magnetic field surrounds an electric current. When charges move, a magnetic field is created. In the previous experiment, you saw that a magnetic field can push on a wire carrying an electric current. Electric motors are based on the principle that a magnetic field will exert a force on a current-carrying wire.

Michael Faraday built the world's first electric motor. It was more a toy than a practical machine. But it was based on the interaction between electric currents and magnets—a new science developed by Faraday, Henry, Oersted, Ampère, and others.

You can apply this principle by building a very simple electric motor. To begin, make a stand for your motor by inverting a Styrofoam cup. Then unfold one end of each of two large paper clips. Tape them to opposite sides of the cup, as shown in Figure 30. Place two disk or rectangular ceramic magnets on top of the inverted cup. Place a third magnet inside the cup and directly beneath the other two. This procedure will add strength to the magnet and help to hold it in place.

The coil, which forms the turning part of the motor, can be made by winding about 30 cm (1 ft) of enamel-coated copper wire three or four times around your first two fingers. Leave some extra wire on each end. Take the coil off your fingers. Wrap the ends around opposite sides of the coil several times to help keep the coil wires in place. Two tiny pieces of tape can be used to hold the wires of the coil in place as shown. The unwrapped end pieces should be about 5 cm (2 in) long. Straighten and then sandpaper these ends to remove the enamel. The sandpapered

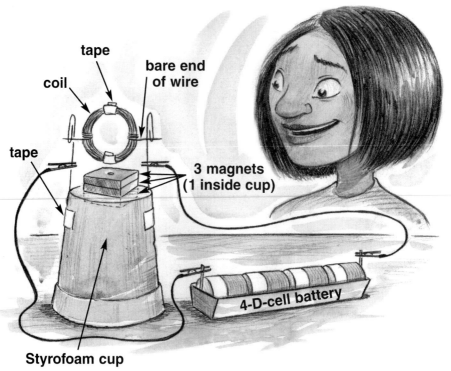

Figure 30.
You can build a simple DC motor.

ends of the coil fit into the loops you made with the paper clips. Turn the coil gently. It should come very close to the top of the magnet. If necessary, adjust the position of the paper clip supports.

Use wires with alligator clips on each end to connect the poles of a 4-D-cell battery or a 6-volt dry cell to the paper clips that support the coil of the motor. Give the coil a gentle flip and watch it spin.

Actually, this motor should not work. Motors that are operated by a battery (DC motors) have a commutator—a device that stops the current in the coil every half turn. Without the commutator, such motors would make only half a turn. Then the force of the magnetic field on the current that you saw in Experiment 5.1 would simply stretch the coil; the coil would not turn any longer.

In the simple motor you made, the coil is so light that it bounces on the paper clip loops and breaks the electrical connection, allowing the coil to rotate past the point where it would simply be stretched.

A MORE COMPLICATED ELECTRIC MOTOR

Ask an adult to use pliers to force a plastic darning or thin knitting needle through the center of a wine cork. **Ask the adult** to also use a sharp knife to cut a V-shaped notch along the sides of the cork. You can then wind 70 turns of thin enamel-coated copper wire around the cork using the notches to support the wire. You have just made what is called the motor's rotor.

Use sandpaper to remove the enamel insulation from about 3 cm (1 in) of each end of the wire coil you have made. Insert a common pin on each side of the coil as shown in Figure 31a. Firmly wind one bared end of wire around one pin and the other bared end around the other pin. The pins and their connections

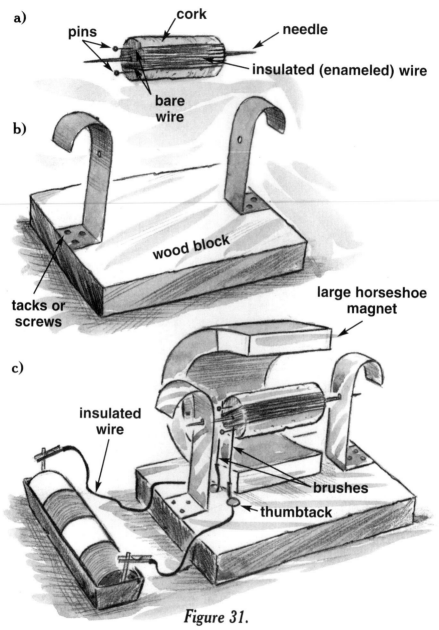

a)

pins

cork

needle

insulated (enameled) wire

bare wire

b)

wood block

tacks or screws

large horseshoe magnet

c)

insulated wire

brushes

thumbtack

Figure 31.

You can build a DC motor with a commutator from simple materials.

to the rotor make up the commutator, an essential part of a DC motor.

Next, build a support for the rotor. **Ask an adult** to cut two 2-cm- (3/4-in-) wide strips from a tin can. The strips should be about twice as long as the cork. Use a hammer and a small nail to punch three holes through one end of each strip. These holes will be used to attach the strip to a wood block, as shown in Figure 31b. Punch another hole through the center of each strip about 4 cm (1.5 in) above the nearest of the three holes you punched before. These holes will support the ends of the darning or knitting needle. Use three tacks or small screws to fix each metal strip to the block of wood. Using pliers, bend the upper ends of each strip into a semicircle as shown. Insert the darning or knitting needle of the rotor through the upper holes in the metal strips. Make sure the rotor turns easily. If it does not, you will have to enlarge the holes.

Make the brushes from two 30-cm (1-ft) pieces of insulated copper wire. Remove about 5 cm (2 in) of insulation from both ends of each wire. Using thumbtacks, fasten each wire to the wooden block so that a bare end of each wire rubs against a commutator pin. Later, you will connect the other ends of the two wires to a 6-volt (4-D-cell) battery.

Put a strong horseshoe magnet in position as shown in Figure 31c. If you do not have such a magnet, you can use ceramic magnets on either side of the coil. Of course, opposite poles of the two magnets should face each other to produce a strong field across the coil. Give the coil a flip and your motor should spin if all connections make contact.

Watch to see which way the motor turns. If you reverse the connections to the battery, does the motor reverse the direction it turns? What happens to the direction the motor turns if you reverse the poles of the magnet?

Science Project Idea

● To understand how important Faraday's discovery was, make a list of all the devices you can think of that use electric motors.

ELECTRIC CURRENTS FROM MAGNETS

Faraday, like most scientists, believed that nature was uniform. Therefore, since an electric current produces a magnetic field, he reasoned a magnetic field should be able to produce an electric current. To test his hypothesis, Faraday placed very strong magnets near and around coils of wire. But nothing happened. There were no electric currents in the coils. He used bigger magnets and more coils of wire; still nothing. Then, on Christmas Day in 1831, Faraday discovered the key to producing a current from magnets. He wrapped a coil of wire around part of an iron ring and connected the coil to a battery. On the other side of the ring, he wrapped another coil of wire and connected it to a meter. When he closed the switch between the battery and the coil, his electric meter revealed that charges flowed, and a momentary current was produced in the other coil. When he opened the switch, the needle moved again, but in the opposite direction.

When he saw the meter's needle move, first one way and then the other, Faraday realized what was needed to generate an electric current from magnets. A steady magnetic field, no matter how big, had no effect on electric charges. What was necessary was a changing magnetic field. Oersted had shown that electric charges must be *moving* to produce a magnetic field. Faraday discovered that a magnetic field had to be *changing* to make electric charges move.

Faraday pictured a magnetic field as lines of force, like those in the pattern made by the iron filings in Experiment 3.2, Figure 20b. He imagined a strong field to consist of many closely packed lines of force. A weak field he thought of as fewer lines less closely packed. Whenever the number of field lines through a coil of wire increased or decreased, electric charges were forced to move. Or, if a wire moved across magnetic field lines, there was a force on charges in the wire.

Experiment 5.3

A Current From a Magnetic Field

Materials

✓ the meter you built in Experiment 4.3

✓ a coil made from 10 m (33 ft) of 24-gauge insulated wire and the core of a roll of duct tape

✓ 2 long insulated wires

✓ strong bar magnet or about 12 ceramic magnets

✓ a partner

✓ strong horseshoe magnet (optional)

A generator based on the principle that Faraday discovered and one that you can build is shown in Figure 32. It consists of two coils, one of which is the meter you built in Experiment 4.3. You will need to build a second identical coil without the compass needle. The second coil should be far enough away from the meter that a magnet has no effect on the meter. You will also need two long insulated wires to connect the ends of the two coils.

You can change the magnetic field through the second or unmetered coil by moving a magnet in and out of the coil. You can use either a strong bar magnet or about six or more ceramic magnets that are joined together. What happens to the meter's needle as you move the magnet in and out of the coil? Which way does the compass needle turn when the south-seeking pole of the

Figure 32.

You can make a simple generator.

magnet is pushed into the coil? Which way does it turn when the magnet is pulled out of the coil? Which way does the compass needle turn when the north-seeking pole is pushed into the coil? Which way does it turn when the magnet is pulled out of the coil?

To change the rate at which the magnetic field changes, you can move the magnet at different speeds. Does the rate at which the magnetic field changes affect the current that is induced? Is there any effect if you do not move the magnet?

Can you generate a current by moving the coil while a partner holds the magnet? Is the induced current affected by the number of turns of wire in the coil? Conduct an experiment to find out.

In Experiment 5.1, you saw that electric charges moving in a wire perpendicular to a magnetic field are pushed in a direction perpendicular to both the field and the current. You might suspect that if you pulled electric charges across a magnetic field there would be a force on those charges. If that force were parallel to the wire, charges within the wire would be forced along it, creating an electric current.

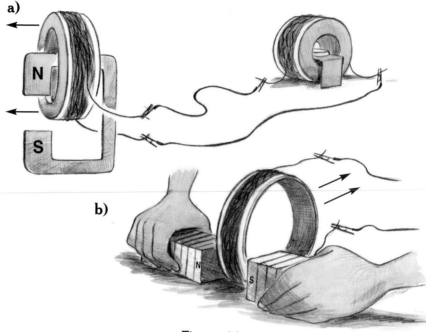

Figure 33.

Does pulling the charges in a wire across a magnetic field cause them to move, creating an electric current? You can find out by using a) a coil and a strong horseshoe magnet, or b) a coil and ceramic magnets held in place by a partner.

To test that idea, connect the unmetered coil to the electric meter with long insulated wires. Be sure the second coil is far enough from the meter that a magnet has no effect on the meter. If you have a large, strong horseshoe magnet, you can pull the coil across the magnetic field as shown in Figure 33a. If you do not have such a magnet, you can use a stack of about a dozen ceramic magnets. Separate the magnets at their center. Have a partner hold the two attracting magnets apart at a distance slightly larger than the width of the coil. Move the coil quickly through the magnetic field as shown in Figure 33b.

Regardless of the magnet you use, what happens as the wires in the coil move across a magnetic field? Is a current induced in the wire? Does pushing the coil into the field have a different effect than pulling the coil out of the field? If it does, can you explain why?

Science Project Idea

- Design and build an electric generator strong enough to light a flashlight bulb.

Chapter 6

Electricity
and
Chemistry

When the telegraph was first used to send messages by wire, a steady source of current was needed. The solution was the Daniell cell, which had been invented in 1836 by an English chemist, John Daniell. A drawing of a Daniell cell is shown in Figure 34. It consists of a large jar, solutions, and electrodes. A solution of a blue compound, copper sulfate, occupies the lower half of the jar. It surrounds a fanlike copper electrode. A less dense solution of zinc sulfate lies above the copper sulfate solution. Suspended inside the zinc sulfate solution is a heavy three-pronged zinc electrode, which was often referred to as a crow's foot. The zinc electrode was large because during the

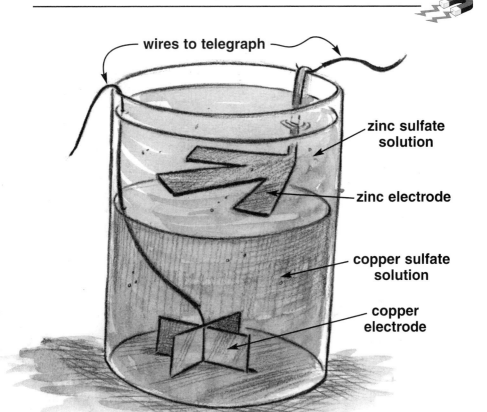

Figure 34.

The drawing shows a Daniell cell. It can supply a steady current for a long time.

chemical reaction that produced an electric current, the zinc dissolved. At the same time, copper collected (plated) on the copper electrode. As zinc atoms dissolved, they released negative charges (electrons). The electrons flowed through the circuit containing the telegraph and back to the copper electrode at the bottom of the cell. There, copper ions (positively charged atoms) in the solution combined with the electrons and plated onto the copper electrode as copper atoms. Because zinc releases negative charges, the zinc is the Daniell cell's negative electrode; the copper is the positive electrode.

You will have an opportunity to see how a Daniell cell works in Experiment 6.1. And, in Experiment 6.2, you will look inside a D cell.

Experiment 6.1

Inside a Daniell Cell

Materials

- ✓ **an adult**
- ✓ safety goggles
- ✓ zinc sulfate ($ZnSO_4 \cdot 7\ H_2O$)
- ✓ metric scale
- ✓ two 1-L flasks
- ✓ water
- ✓ baby food jars

- ✓ paper towel
- ✓ strips of copper and zinc 4 cm x 1 cm (1.6 in x 0.4 in)
- ✓ copper sulfate ($CuSO_4 \cdot 5H_2O$)
- ✓ insulated wires
- ✓ galvanometer or electric meter from Experiment 4.3

In this experiment you will be working with chemicals. Be sure to **wear safety goggles and work under adult supervision**. Also, be sure to **wash your hands thoroughly afterward**. It will help you to keep written notes of the many quick experiments you will be doing with chemicals.

To keep a Daniell cell working for long periods of time, it was essential that the solutions and electrodes be kept apart. Even though the solutions were in contact, there was very little mixing. The copper sulfate was denser than the zinc sulfate, so it tended to remain at the bottom of the jar. Furthermore, when the cell was providing a current, copper ions kept moving toward the copper electrode.

You will use copper sulfate and zinc sulfate solutions in these experiments. To prepare the zinc sulfate solution, add 25 g of zinc sulfate ($ZnSO_4 \cdot 7\ H_2O$) to 1 liter of water and stir. To prepare the copper sulfate solution, add 25 g of copper sulfate ($CuSO_4 \cdot 5\ H_2O$) to 1 liter of water and stir.

To see why the solutions and electrodes in the Daniell cell were kept apart, dip a strip of copper into a baby food jar that contains some copper sulfate solution. Leave it for about a minute. Then remove it. Did anything happen to the copper strip?

Rinse the copper strip in water. Then dip it in some zinc sulfate solution for a minute. Did anything happen? What would happen if zinc sulfate solution reached the copper electrode?

Is there any noticeable reaction if you place a zinc strip in a zinc sulfate solution? Rinse the zinc strip in water. Then place it in copper sulfate solution for a minute. What do you observe? What happens if you leave the copper in the zinc sulfate for several minutes? If you leave it overnight? What would

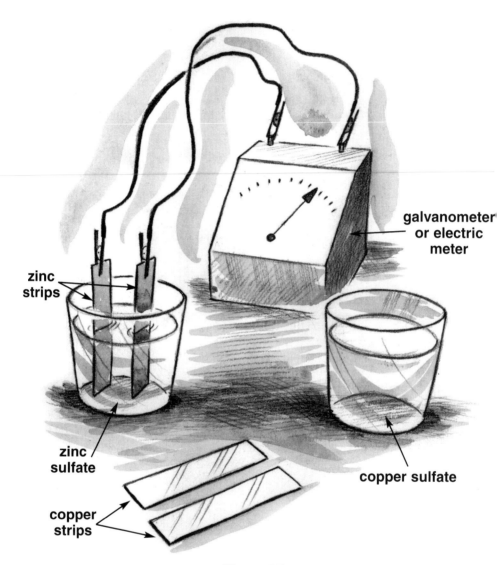

zinc
strips

galvanometer
or electric
meter

zinc
sulfate

copper sulfate

copper
strips

Figure 35.

Will zinc strips in zinc sulfate produce a current? How about copper strips in copper sulfate? How about a copper strip in copper sulfate and a zinc strip in zinc sulfate?

eventually happen to the zinc electrode in a Daniell cell if it were in contact with copper sulfate?

Use insulated wires to connect two zinc strips to your electric meter or to a galvanometer. Dip both strips into a baby food jar containing zinc sulfate solution as shown in Figure 35. Is any current produced?

After rinsing the zinc strips, dip them both into a solution of copper sulfate solution. Is there any current?

Next, connect two copper strips to your electric meter or to a galvanometer. Dip both strips into a baby food jar containing zinc sulfate solution. Is any current produced? After rinsing the copper strips, dip them both into a solution of copper sulfate solution. Is there any current?

Now connect a zinc strip and a copper strip to the galvanometer or to your electric meter. Is there a current when you dip these strips into zinc sulfate? Is there a current when you dip these strips into copper sulfate?

Finally, connect a zinc strip and a copper strip to the galvanometer or to your electric meter. Place the zinc strip in a solution of zinc sulfate. In a separate jar, place the copper strip in a copper sulfate solution. Is there any current? Now connect the two solutions with a paper towel strip as shown in Figure 36. What happens when the two solutions diffuse along the towel and meet?

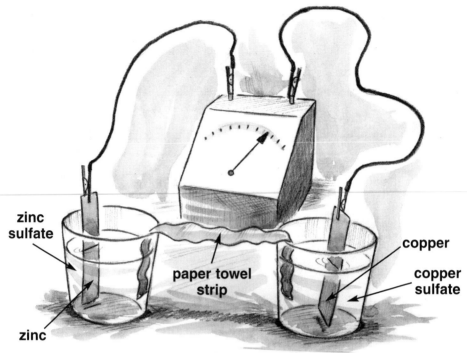

Figure 36.

What is the purpose of the paper towel? Will there be a current without it?

Science Project Idea

● Your science teacher may be able to help you obtain a Daniell cell. Figure out a way to place the copper sulfate solution below the zinc sulfate solution without mixing them. Connect the cell to a low-wattage bulb in series with an ammeter. What current flows? For how long will the cell provide current for the lightbulb?

Experiment 6.2

Inside a D cell

Materials

✓ **an adult**

✓ D cell

✓ hacksaw

✓ electric meter from Experiment 4.3

A Daniell cell, like all electric cells, has two electrodes and an electrolyte. The electrolyte is a liquid or a damp solid through which charges can move. As you saw in Experiment 6.1, charges must be able to flow within the cell as well as outside. The electrolyte makes this possible. When the copper sulfate and zinc sulfate solutions were separated, no current could flow. Connecting them with a wet paper towel provided a bridge through which charges could move from one electrode to the other.

Ordinary D cells, which are used in flashlights, are quite different than Daniell cells. To see what is inside a D cell, **ask an adult** to use a hacksaw to cut a D cell in half lengthwise, as shown in Figure 37. The black rod extending through the center of the cell is the positive electrode. The zinc can, which is insulated from the carbon rod, is the negative electrode, just as it was in the Daniell cell. The electrolyte is a moist black mixture of carbon powder, manganese dioxide, and ammonium chloride.

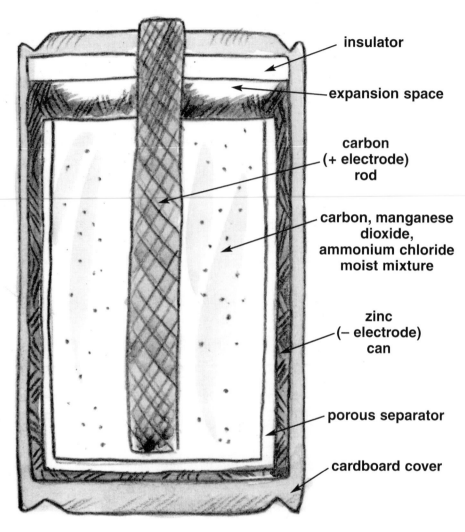

insulator

expansion space

carbon
(+ electrode)
rod

carbon, manganese
dioxide,
ammonium chloride
moist mixture

zinc
(– electrode)
can

porous separator

cardboard cover

Figure 37.

The diagram shows a D cell cut in half. Not all D cells have a cardboard cover. A carbon rod is the positive electrode. The zinc can is the negative electrode. A moist mixture of carbon, manganese dioxide, and ammonium chloride serves as the electrolyte.

The porous separator allows ammonium chloride to reach the zinc can but prevents manganese dioxide and carbon from making contact with the zinc.

Using the ends of the two wires from the electric meter you made in Experiment 4.3, touch the carbon rod in two different places. Does a current flow when you do this? Does a current flow when you touch the carbon rod and the zinc can? Will there be a current if you touch the zinc can and the black electrolyte? How about if you touch the carbon rod and the electrolyte?

Why do you think D cells are often called dry cells?

Science Project Ideas

- Which parts of the D cell do you think will conduct an electric current? Design an experiment to find out.

- Some people keep electric cells, such as D cells, in their refrigerator. Do D cells have a longer shelf life if kept cool? Design an experiment to find out.

Experiment 6.3

The Minimum Ingredients for an Electric Cell

Materials

✓ zinc and copper strips

✓ an olive

✓ insulated wires

✓ a lemon

✓ galvanometer and/or microammeter

✓ copper, aluminum, and steel nails

✓ electric meter from Experiment 4.3

✓ various fruits

✓ steel wool

✓ 3 copper pennies

✓ 3 steel washers

✓ blotter paper

✓ scissors

✓ salt

✓ water

✓ cup

✓ clothespins

As you have seen, an electric cell needs two different electrodes and an electrolyte. Even nails or strips of two different metals stuck in a piece of fruit can act as an electric cell. To see that this is true, push a zinc strip and a copper strip into an olive. Be sure the strips are close together. Use insulated wires to connect the metal strips to the electric meter you built in Experiment 4.3 or to a galvanometer. Does a current flow?

Repeat the experiment using a lemon. If you do not obtain a current, try squeezing the lemon to break up the internal sections. If you still cannot detect a current, connect the electrodes to a galvanometer or to a microammeter, which measures millionths of an ampere.

If placed in an olive, will a copper and an aluminum nail produce a current? A steel and a copper nail? A steel and an aluminum nail? How about two copper nails?

Can other fruits also serve as electrolytes? Design experiments to find out.

THE FIRST ELECTRIC CELL

Luigi Galvani was an eighteenth-century Italian scientist who taught anatomy to medical students. Galvani discovered that if he touched a frog's leg with two different metals, the leg would twitch. Galvani thought that the electricity came from the frog. Another eighteenth-century Italian scientist, Alessandro Volta, thought the electricity involved the interaction of the two different metals.

To show that the electricity came from the two different metals, Volta built a battery. He placed disks of copper and zinc alternately in a stack with cardboard soaked in saltwater between them. Volta had made the world's first battery, which produced a direct current.

You can make a simple battery like Volta's. Use steel wool to polish three copper pennies and three steel washers so that they are shiny. Cut blotter paper into circles that are slightly larger than the pennies and washers. Soak the paper circles in a concentrated solution of salt and water. Make a paper "sandwich" by placing the wet paper between a penny and a washer as shown in Figure 38a. Hold the sandwich together with a clothespin. Touch the ends of the wires from your electric meter to the electric cell as shown. Does the meter indicate a current? If not, make the stack larger by adding in alternate fashion penny, wet paper, steel washer until you have a 3-cell battery as shown in Figure 38b. Test this battery with your electric meter. Is the current detectable? If not, try testing with a galvanometer or a microammeter.

What are the electrodes in this simple battery? What is the electrolyte?

Science Project Ideas

- You may have seen science books that show a flashlight bulb being lighted by a lemon. Is this possible? Design an experiment to find out.

- Investigate the corrosion of metals. How is corrosion related to electric cells?

- Build the electrical instrument that was named for Galvani.

- Build the electrical meter that was named for Volta and explain how it works.

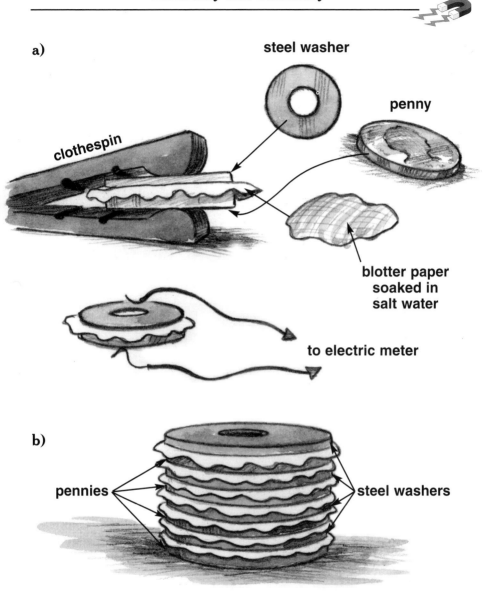

Figure 38.

a) Make an electric cell from a penny, a steel washer, and a blotter-paper disk soaked in salt solution. Test this cell with your electric meter. b) Make a battery by stacking three cells together.

By now you have seen that electric charges can be at rest, as they are in a cloud. Or they can be moving, as they are when an electric current flows. The world's largest electric currents occur when the attraction between static charges of opposite sign (+ and −) in clouds or between clouds and the ground becomes so large that the charges flow through the air. We call this huge current lightning.

More useful and far less dangerous currents are produced by the batteries and generators you have investigated. These currents are used to light our homes, schools, and industries; turn our many electric motors; and run our electronic devices such as computers.

The similarity between electricity and magnetism, which for many centuries could not be explained, is no longer a mystery to you. You have seen how magnetic fields arise from electric currents and how changing magnetic fields can induce electric currents. Along the way, you have learned how to build simple switches, electric meters and motors, electromagnets, electric cells, as well as how to plate metals and send messages using electricity.

Many of the mysteries about electricity and magnetism are no longer so mysterious. Your experiments have answered many questions. But there is much more to learn. What you have discovered here may inspire you to continue with further study of the fascinating subject of electricity and magnetism.

Appendix

SCIENCE SUPPLY COMPANIES

Carolina Biological Supply Company
2700 York Road
Burlington, NC 27215-3398
(800) 334-5551
http://www.carolina.com

Connecticut Valley Biological
Supply Company
82 Valley Road
P.O. Box 326
Southampton, MA 01073
(800) 628-7748
http://www.ctvalleybio.com

Delta Education
80 Northwest Boulevard
P.O. Box 3000
Nashua, NH 03061-3000
(800) 442-5444
http://www.delta-education.com

Educational Innovations, Inc.
362 Main Avenue
Norwalk, CT 06851
(888) 912-7474
http://www.teachersource.com

Fisher Science Education
4500 Turnberry Drive
Hanover Park, IL 60133
(800) 955-1177
http://www.fisheredu.com

Frey Scientific
100 Paragon Parkway
Mansfield, OH 44903
(800) 225-3739
http://www.freyscientific.com/

NASCO-Fort Atkinson
901 Janesville Avenue
P.O. Box 901
Fort Atkinson, WI 53538-0901
(800) 558-9595
http://www.nascofa.com/

NASCO-Modesto
4825 Stoddard Road
P.O. Box 3837
Modesto, CA 95352-3837
(800) 558-9595
http://www.nascofa.com

Sargent-Welch/VWR Scientific
P.O. Box 5229
Buffalo Grove, IL 60089-5229
(800) 727-4386
http://www.sargentwelch.com

Science Kit & Boreal Laboratories
777 East Park Drive
P.O. Box 5003
Tonawanda, NY 14150
(800) 828-7777
http://sciencekit.com

Ward's Natural Science
P.O. Box 92912
Rochester, NY 14692-9012
(800) 962-2660
http://www.wardsci.com

Further Reading

Ardley, Neil, and Jack Challoner. *Electricity*. Orlando, Fla.: Raintree Steck-Vaughn, 2000.

Fleisher, Paul. Waves: *Principles of Light, Electricity, and Magnetism*. Minneapolis, Minn.: Lerner Publishing Group, 2001.

Gardner, Robert. *Science Projects About Methods of Measuring*. Berkeley Heights, N.J.: Enslow Publishers, Inc., 2000.

_____. *Science Fair Projects: Planning, Preparing, Succeeding*. Springfield, N.J.: Enslow Publishers, Inc., 1998.

Parker, Steve. *Electricity*. New York: Dorling Kindersley Publishing, 2000.

Tocci, Salvatore. *How to Do a Science Fair Project, Revised Edition*. Danbury, Conn.: Franklin Watts, 1997.

Wood, Robert W. *Electricity and Magnetism*. Broomall, Penn.: Chelsea House, 1999.

Internet Addresses

The Exploratorium:
http://www.exploratorium.edu

The Franklin Institute Online:
http://www.fi.edu/qa97/spotlight3/spotlight3.html

Index